T3-BHN-630

Fodor's ® New FIRST EDITION
Pocket Berlin

Excerpted from *Fodor's Germany*

Fodor's Travel Publications, Inc.
New York • Toronto • London • Sydney • Auckland
www.fodors.com

Fodor's Pocket Berlin

EDITORS: Christina Knight, Alison Stern

Editorial Contributors: David Brown, Helayne Schiff, Jürgen Scheunemann, M. T. Schwartzmann (Essential Information editor)

Editorial Production: Linda K. Schmidt

Maps: David Lindroth, *cartographer;* Steven Amsterdam and Robert Blake, *map editors*

Design: Fabrizio La Rocca, *creative director;* Guido Caroti, *associate art director;* Lyndell Brookhouse-Gil, *cover designer;* Jolie Novak, *photo editor*

Production/Manufacturing: Rebecca Zeiler

Cover Photograph: Canard/Tony Stone Images

Copyright

Special Sales

Fodor's Travel Publications are available at special discounts for bulk purchases for sales promotions or premiums. Special editions, including personalized covers, excerpts of existing guides, and corporate imprints, can be created in large quantities for special needs. For more information, contact your local bookseller or write to Special Markets, Fodor's Travel Publications, 201 East 50th Street, New York, NY 10022. Inquiries from Canada should be directed to your local Canadian bookseller or sent to Random House of Canada, Ltd., Marketing Department, 2775 Matheson Boulevard East, Mississauga, Ontario L4W 4P7. Inquiries from the United Kingdom should be sent to Fodor's Travel Publications, 20 Vauxhall Bridge Road, London SW1V 2SA, England.

PRINTED IN THE UNITED STATES OF AMERICA

10 9 8 7 6 5 4 3 2 1

CONTENTS

On the Road with Fodor's   v

About Our Writer *v*
Connections *v*
How to Use This Book *vi*
Don't Forget to Write *vii*

Essential Information   *xii*

1   ## Destination: Berlin   *1*

Berlin on the Cutting Edge *2*
Pleasures and Pastimes *4*
Half-Day Itineraries *5*

2   ## Exploring Berlin   9

3   ## Dining   38

4   ## Lodging   46

5   ## Nightlife and the Arts   55

6   ## Outdoor Activities and Sports   65

7   ## Shopping   68

8   ## Side Trips from Berlin   75

Potsdam *76*
Frankfurt an der Oder *84*

German Vocabulary   86

Menu Guide   89

Index   97

Maps

Germany *viii–ix*
Berlin Public Transit
  Sytem *x–xi*
Berlin Exploring *12–13*

Berlin Dining *42–43*
Berlin Lodging *48–49*
Berlin Side Trips *78–79*

ON THE ROAD WITH FODOR'S

WHEN I PLAN a vacation, the first thing I do is cast around among my friends and colleagues to find someone who's just been where I'm going. That's because there's no substitute for a recommendation from a good friend who knows your tastes, your budget, and your circumstances, someone who's just been there. Unfortunately, such friends are few and far between. So it's nice to know that there's *Fodor's Pocket Berlin*.

In the first place, this book won't stay home when you hit the road. It will accompany you every step of the way, steering you away from wrong turns and wrong choices and never expecting a thing in return. Most important of all, it's written and assiduously updated by the kind of people you *would* hit up for travel tips if you knew them. Fodor's writers are as choosy as your pickiest friend, except they've probably seen a lot more of Berlin. We don't send you chasing down every sight, but instead have selected the best ones, the ones that are worthy of your time and money. To make it easy for you to put it all together in the time you have, we've created half-day itineraries that you can mix and match in a snap.

About Our Writer

Our success in achieving our goals and in helping to make your trip the best of all possible vacations is a credit to the hard work of our writers and updaters over the years.

Berlin resident **Jürgen Scheunemann** fell in love with Berlin 11 years ago when he moved to there to study North American history and German literature. Since then, Jürgen has worked as a professional journalist, editor, and book writer. Among other assignments, he was a contract writer for Berlin's leading daily, *Der Tagesspiegel;* worked for the *BBC Television London;* and wrote, published, and translated a number of books on Berlin and the United States. He is currently doing research for his Ph.D. in American history.

Connections

We're pleased that the American Society of Travel Agents continues to endorse Fodor's as its guidebook of choice. ASTA is the world's largest and most influential travel trade association, operating in more than 170 countries, with 27,000 members pledged to adhere to a strict code of ethics reflecting the Society's motto, "Integrity in Travel." ASTA shares Fodor's devotion to providing smart, honest travel information and advice to travelers, and we've long recommended that our readers—even those who have guidebooks and traveling friends—consult ASTA member agents for the experience and professionalism they bring to your vacation planning.

On Fodor's Web site (www. fodors.com), check out the new Resource Center, an on-line companion to the Essential Information of this book, complete with useful hot links to related sites. In our forums, you can also get lively advice from other travelers and more great tips from Fodor's experts worldwide.

How to Use This Book

Organization

Up front is **Essential Information,** an easy-to-use section divided alphabetically by topic. Under each listing you'll find tips, addresses, and phone numbers of organizations and companies that offer destination-related services and detailed information and publications.

The first chapter in the guide, Destination: Berlin, gets you into the mood for your trip. Pleasures and Pastimes describes the activities and sights that make Berlin unique, and Half-Day Itineraries lays out a selection of complete trips. The Exploring chapter is divided into geographic areas and lists sights within them alphabetically. The remaining chapters are arranged in alphabetical order by subject (dining, lodging, nightlife and the arts, outdoor activities and sports, shopping, and side trips). German vocabulary and a menu guide precede the index.

Icons and Symbols

★ Our special recommendations
✕ Restaurant
🏨 Lodging establishment
🐣 Good for kids (rubber duckie)
☞ Sends you to another section for more information
⊠ Address
☎ Telephone number
🕓 Opening and closing times
💰 Admission prices (those we give apply to adults; substantially reduced fees are almost always available for children, students, and senior citizens)

Hotel Facilities

We always list the facilities that are available—but we don't specify whether they cost extra: When pricing accommodations, always ask what's included. In addition, assume that all rooms have private baths unless otherwise noted.

Restaurant Reservations and Dress Codes

Reservations are always a good idea; we note only when they're essential or when they're not accepted. Book as far ahead as you can, and be sure to reconfirm. Unless otherwise noted, the restaurants listed are open daily for lunch and dinner. We mention dress only when men must wear a jacket or a jacket and tie.

Credit Cards

The following abbreviations are used: **AE**, American Express; **D**, Discover; **DC**, Diners Club; **MC**, MasterCard; and **V**, Visa.

Don't Forget to Write

You can use this book in the confidence that all prices and opening times are based on information supplied to us at press time; Fodor's cannot accept responsibility for any errors. Time inevitably brings changes, so always confirm information when it matters—especially if you're making a detour to visit a specific place.

Were the restaurants we recommended as described? Did our hotel picks exceed your expectations? Did you find a museum we recommended a waste of time? Keeping a travel guide fresh and up-to-date is a big job, and we welcome your feedback, positive *and* negative. If you have complaints, we'll look into them and revise our entries when the facts warrant it. If you've discovered a special place that we haven't included, we'll pass the information along to our correspondents and have them check it out. So send us your thoughts via e-mail at editors@fodors.com (specifying the name of the book on the subject line) or on paper in care of the *Pocket Berlin* editor at Fodor's, 201 East 50th Street, New York, New York 10022. In the meantime, have a wonderful trip!

Karen Cure

Karen Cure
Editorial Director

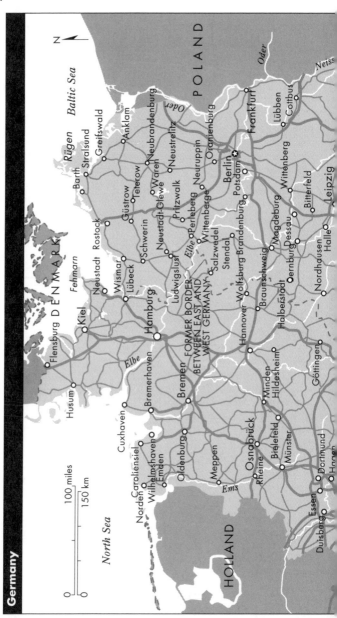

Germany

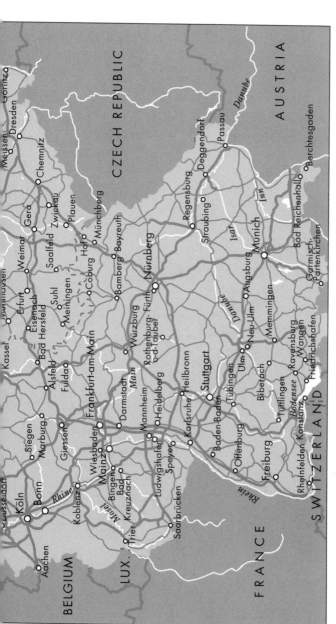

Berlin Public Transit System

U1 U-Bahn
S1 S-Bahn

ESSENTIAL INFORMATION

Basic Information on Traveling in Berlin, Savvy Tips to Make Your Trip a Breeze, and Companies and Organizations to Contact

ADDRESSES

Even eight years after the official unification of the two Berlins, the nuts-and-bolts work of joining up the halves is not complete, and massive construction adds to the flux. We have given addresses, telephone numbers, and other logistical details based on the best available information, but please understand that everything from telephone numbers to street names are still changing at a furious pace. Inquire at one of Berlin's tourist information offices for the most up-to-date information.

AIR TRAVEL

BOOKING YOUR FLIGHT

Not many airlines have nonstop flights to Berlin, and fares to Berlin are usually higher than to other German cities like Frankfurt. U.S. airlines often connect to other carriers like Lufthansa or Swiss Air to complete legs of the flight.

Price is just one factor to consider when booking a flight: frequency of service and even a carrier's safety record are often just as important. Major airlines offer the greatest number of departures. Smaller airlines—including regional and no-frills airlines—usually have a limited number of flights daily. On the other hand, so-called low-cost airlines usually are cheaper, and their fares impose fewer restrictions, such as advance-purchase requirements. Safety-wise, low-cost carriers as a group have a good history—about equal to that of major carriers.

When you book, **look for nonstop flights** and **remember that "direct" flights stop at least once.** Try to **avoid connecting flights,** which require a change of plane. International flights on a country's flag carrier are almost always nonstop.

CARRIERS

When flying internationally, you must usually choose between a domestic carrier, the national flag carrier of the country you are visiting, and a foreign carrier from a third country. National flag carriers have the greatest number of nonstops. Domestic carriers may have better connections to your home town and serve a greater number of gateway cities. Third-party carriers may have a price advantage.

➤ MAJOR AIRLINES: **American** (☎ 800/433–7300) usually connects via London. **Continental**

(☎ 800/231–0856) connects via Paris. **Delta** (☎ 800/221–1212) connects via Zurich. **LTU International Airways** (☎ 800/888–0200) connects via Dusseldorf. **Lufthansa** (☎ 800/645–3880) has nonstop flights. **Northwest** (☎ 800/225–2525). **TWA** (☎ 800/221–2000) connects via Paris. **United** (☎ 800/538–2929) connects via Dusseldorf or Frankfurt.

➤ FROM THE U.K.: **British Airways** (☎ 0345/222–111), **Lufthansa** (✉ 10 Old Bond St., London W1X 4EN, ☎ 0181/750–3300 or 0345/737–747), and **Air UK** (☎ 0345/666–777).

CHARTERS

Charters usually have the lowest fares but are the least dependable. Departures are infrequent and seldom on time, flights can be delayed for up to 48 hours or can be canceled for any reason up to 10 days before you're scheduled to leave. Itineraries and prices can change after you've booked your flight.

In the U.S., the Department of Transportation's Aviation Consumer Protection Division has jurisdiction over charters and provides a certain degree of protection. The DOT requires that money paid to charter operators be held in escrow, so if you can't pay with a credit card, **always make your check payable to a charter carrier's escrow account.** The name of the bank should be

in the charter contract. If you have any problems with a charter operator, contact the DOT (☞ Airline Complaints, *below*). If you buy a charter package that includes both air and land arrangements, remember that the escrow requirement applies only to the air component.

CONSOLIDATORS

Consolidators buy tickets for scheduled international flights at reduced rates from the airlines, then sell them at prices that beat the best fare available directly from the airlines, usually without restrictions. Sometimes you can even get your money back if you need to return the ticket. Carefully read the fine print detailing penalties for changes and cancellations, and **confirm your consolidator reservation with the airline.**

➤ CONSOLIDATORS: **Cheap Tickets** (☎ 800/377–1000). **Up & Away Travel** (☎ 212/889–2345). **Discount Travel Network** (☎ 800/576–1600). **Unitravel** (☎ 800/325–2222). **World Travel Network** (☎ 800/409–6753).

COURIERS

When you fly as a courier, you trade your checked-luggage space for a ticket subsidized by a courier service. It's all perfectly legitimate, but there are restrictions: You can usually book your flight only a week or two in advance, your length of stay may be set for a certain number of days, and you probably won't be able to book a companion on the same flight.

CUTTING COSTS

The least-expensive airfares to Berlin are priced for round-trip travel and usually must be purchased in advance. It's smart to **call a number of airlines, and when you are quoted a good price, book it on the spot**—the same fare may not be available the next day. Airlines generally allow you to change your return date for a fee. If you don't use your ticket, you can apply the cost toward the purchase of a new ticket, again for a small charge. However, most low-fare tickets are nonrefundable. To get the lowest airfare, **check different routings.** Compare prices of flights to and from different airports if your destination or home city has more than one gateway. Also price off-peak flights, which may be significantly less expensive.

Travel agents, especially those who specialize in finding the lowest fares (☞ Discounts & Deals, *below*), can be especially helpful when booking a plane ticket. When you're quoted a price, **ask your agent if the price is likely to get any lower.** Good agents know the seasonal fluctuations of airfares and can usually anticipate a sale or fare war. However, waiting can be risky: The fare could go *up* as seats become scarce, or you may wait so long that your preferred flight sells out. A wait-and-see strategy works best if your plans are flexible. If you must arrive and depart on certain dates, don't delay.

CHECK IN & BOARDING

Airlines routinely overbook planes, assuming that not everyone with a ticket will show up, but sometimes everyone does. When that happens, airlines ask for volunteers to give up their seats. In return these volunteers usually get a certificate for a free flight and are rebooked on the next flight out. If there are not enough volunteers, the airline must choose who will be denied boarding. The first to get bumped are passengers who checked in late and those flying on discounted tickets, so **get to the gate and check in as early as possible,** especially during peak periods.

Although the trend on international flights is to drop reconfirmation requirements, many airlines still ask you to reconfirm each leg of your international itinerary. Failure to do so may result in your reservation being canceled.

Always **bring a government-issued photo ID to the airport.** You may be asked to show it before you are allowed to check in.

ENJOYING THE FLIGHT

For more legroom, **request an emergency-aisle seat.** Don't sit in the row in front of the emergency aisle or in front of a bulkhead, where seats may not recline.

If you don't like airline food, **ask for special meals when booking.** These can be vegetarian, low-cholesterol, or kosher, for example.

When flying internationally, try to maintain a normal routine, to help fight jet-lag. At night, **get some sleep.** By day, **eat light meals, drink water (not alcohol), and move around the cabin** to stretch your legs.

Many carriers have prohibited smoking on all of their international flights; others allow smoking only on certain routes or certain departures, so **contact your carrier regarding its smoking policy.**

FLYING TIMES

A journey to Berlin is usually long because most flights are not direct. Travel time will depend on where your connection is made and how long your layover is. For instance, Berlin is approximately a 1 hour and 45 minute flight from either London or Paris, and a 1-hour flight from Frankfurt.

HOW TO COMPLAIN

If your baggage goes astray or your flight goes awry, complain right away. Most carriers require that you **file a claim immediately.**

➤ AIRLINE COMPLAINTS: U.S. Department of Transportation **Aviation Consumer Protection Division** (✉ C-75, Room 4107, Washington, DC 20590, ☎ 202/366–2220). **Federal Aviation** Administration Consumer Hotline (☎ 800/322–7873).

AIRPORTS

Tegel is the main airport and **Templehof**, which at press time was still serving smaller German cities, is likely to close in 1999.

➤ MAIN AIRPORT: **Flughafen Tegel** (☎ 011–49–30/69510 (general information) or 011–49/180–500–0186 (arrival and departure hotline).

AIRPORT TRANSFERS

Tegel Airport is only 6 km (4 mi) from the downtown area. The No. 109 and X09 airport buses run at 10-minute intervals between Tegel and downtown via Kurfürstendamm (downtown western Berlin), Bahnhof Zoologischer Garten, and Budapester Strasse. The trip takes 30 minutes; the fare is DM 3.90. Expect to pay about DM 25 for the same trip by taxi. If you rent a car at the airport, take the Stadtautobahn (there are signs) into Berlin. The Halensee exit leads to Kurfürstendamm.

BIKES IN FLIGHT

Most airlines will accommodate bikes as luggage, provided they are dismantled and put into a box. Call to see if your airline sells bike boxes (about $5; bike bags are at least $100), although you can often pick them up free at bike shops. International travelers can sometimes substitute a bike for a piece of checked luggage for free;

otherwise, it will cost about $100. Domestic and Canadian airlines charge a $25–$50 fee.

BUSINESS HOURS

BANKS

Banks are generally open weekdays from 8:30 or 9 to 2 or 3 (5 or 6 on Thursday), with a lunch break of about an hour. Branches at airports and main train stations open as early as 6:30 AM and close as late as 10:30 PM.

MUSEUMS

Several museums are undergoing renovations in 1999, including some on Museum Island; some exhibition halls may be closed or hours may be changed. Most museums are open from Tuesday to Sunday 9–6. Some close for an hour or more at lunch, and some are open on Monday. Many stay open late on Wednesday or Thursday.

SHOPS

Department stores and larger shops are generally open 9 or 9:15–8 PM weekdays and until 2 PM on Saturday. Some smaller shops stay open until 4 PM on Saturday.

CAMERAS & COMPUTERS

EQUIPMENT PRECAUTIONS

Always **keep your film, tape, or computer disks out of the sun.** Carry an extra supply of batteries, and **be prepared to turn on your camera, camcorder, or laptop** to prove to security personnel that the device is real. Always **ask for hand inspection of film,** which becomes clouded after successive exposure to airport X-ray machines, and **keep videotapes and computer disks away from metal detectors.**

TRAVEL PHOTOGRAPHY

➤ PHOTO HELP: **Kodak Information Center** (☎ 800/242–2424). *Kodak Guide to Shooting Great Travel Pictures,* available in bookstores or from Fodor's Travel Publications (☎ 800/533–6478; $16.50 plus $4 shipping).

CAR RENTAL

Tax on car rentals is 16%. Note that you cannot drive a car rented in Germany into Poland; check with the rental agency for other travel restrictions.

➤ MAJOR AGENCIES: **Avis** (☎ 800/331–1084, 800/879–2847 in Canada, 008/225–533 in Australia). **Budget** (☎ 800/527–0700, 0800/181181 in the U.K.). **Hertz** (☎ 800/654–3001, 800/263–0600 in Canada, 0345/555888 in the U.K., 03/9222–2523 in Australia, 03/358–6777 in New Zealand).

➤ WITHIN BERLIN: **Avis:** ⊠ Tegel Airport, ☎ 030/4101–3148; ⊠ Budapester Str. 43, Am Europa Center, ☎ 030/2309–370; ⊠ Karl-Marx-Allee 264, ☎ 030/685–2093. **Europcar:** ⊠ Tegel Airport, ☎ 030/4101–3354; ⊠ Kurfürsten-str. 101, ☎ 030/2350–640. **Hertz:** ⊠ Tegel Airport, ☎ 030/4101–3315; ⊠ Budapester Str. 39,

☏ 030/261–1053. **SixtBudget:** ✉ Tegel Airport, ☏ 030/4101–2886; ✉ Nürnberger Str. 65, ☏ 030/ 2129–8811.

CUTTING COSTS

To get the best deal, **book through a travel agent who is willing to shop around.**

Also **ask your travel agent about a company's customer-service record.** How has the company responded to late plane arrivals and vehicle mishaps? Are there often lines at the rental counter? If you're traveling during a holiday period, does a confirmed reservation guarantee you a car?

Be sure to **look into wholesalers,** companies that do not own fleets but rent in bulk from those that do and often offer better rates than traditional car-rental operations. Prices are best during off-peak periods. Rentals booked through wholesalers must be paid for before you leave the United States.

➤ RENTAL WHOLESALERS: **Auto Europe** (☏ 207/842–2000 or 800/223–5555, ℻ 800/235–6321). **Europe by Car** (☏ 212/ 581–3040 or 800/223–1516, ℻ 212/246–1458). **DER Travel Services** (✉ 9501 W. Devon Ave., Rosemont, IL 60018, ☏ 800/ 782–2424, ℻ 800/282–7474 for information or 800/860–9944 for brochures). **Kemwel Holiday Autos** (☏ 914/835–5555 or 800/ 678–0678, ℻ 914/835–5126).

INSURANCE

When driving a rented car you are generally responsible for any damage to or loss of the vehicle. Collision policies that car-rental companies sell for European rentals typically do not cover stolen vehicles. Before you buy additional insurance, **see what coverage you already have** under the terms of your personal auto-insurance policy and credit cards—you may already be covered.

REQUIREMENTS

In Germany your own driver's license is acceptable, but an International Driver's Permit is a good idea; it's available from the American or Canadian automobile association, and, in the United Kingdom, from the Automobile Association or Royal Automobile Club. These international permits are universally recognized, and having one in your wallet may save you a problem with the local authorities.

SURCHARGES

Before you pick up a car in one city and leave it in another, **ask about drop-off charges or one-way service fees,** which can be substantial. Note, too, that some rental agencies charge extra if you return the car before the time specified in your contract. To avoid a hefty refueling fee, **fill the tank just before you turn in the car,** but be aware that gas stations near the rental outlet may overcharge.

CAR TRAVEL

The "transit corridor" roads linking former West Germany with Berlin are still there, but the strict restrictions that once confined foreign motorists driving through East Germany have vanished, and today you can travel through the country at will. Expressways link Berlin with the eastern German cities of Magdeburg, Leipzig, Rostock, Dresden, and Frankfurt an der Oder. At press time speed restrictions of 130 kph (80 mph) still applied, and you must carry your driver's license, car registration, and insurance documents with you. Seat belts must be worn at all times, even in the backseat.

Berliners are famous for their reckless driving, so exploring the city by car can be extremely frustrating for out-of-towners. Due to the many construction sites, traffic on many streets is often detoured, and business traffic in the morning and late afternoon hours is stop-and-go for every driver. It's best to leave your car at the hotel and take the public transit system.

AUTO CLUBS

➤ IN GERMANY: There are three principal automobile clubs in Germany: **ADAC** (Allgemeiner Deutscher Automobil-Club, ✉ Am Westpark 8, D–81373 Munich, ☎ 089/76760), **AvD** (Automobilclub von Deutschland, ✉ Lyonerstr. 16, D–60528 Frankfurt, ☎ 069/66060), and **DTC** (Deutscher Touring-Automobil Club, ✉ Amalienburgstr. 23, D–81247 Munich, ☎ 089/891–1330).

➤ IN AUSTRALIA: **Australian Automobile Association** (☎ 06/247–7311).

➤ IN CANADA: **Canadian Automobile Association** (CAA, ☎ 613/247–0117).

➤ IN NEW ZEALAND: **New Zealand Automobile Association** (☎ 09/377–4660).

➤ IN THE U.K.: **Automobile Association** (AA, ☎ 0990/500–600), **Royal Automobile Club** (RAC, ☎ 0990/722–722 for membership, 0345/121–345 for insurance).

➤ IN THE U.S.: **American Automobile Association** (☎ 800/564–6222).

EMERGENCY SERVICES

ADAC and AvD (☞ Auto Clubs, *above*) operate tow trucks on all autobahns; they also have emergency telephones every 3 km (2 mi). On minor roads, **go to the nearest call box and dial 01802/222–222.** Ask, in English, for road service assistance. Help is free (with the exception of all materials) if the work is carried out by the ADAC. If the ADAC has to use a subcontactor for the work, charges are made for time, mileage, and materials.

FROM THE U.K.

It is recommended that drivers **get a green card** from their insurance companies, which extends insurance coverage to driving in continental Europe. Extra breakdown insurance and vehicle and personal security coverage is also advisable.

GASOLINE

Gasoline (petrol) costs are between DM 1.20 and DM 1.70 per liter. As part of antipollution efforts, most German cars now run on lead-free fuel and leaded gas is becoming more and more difficult to find. Some models use diesel fuel, so if you are renting a car, **find out which fuel the car takes.** Some older vehicles cannot take unleaded fuel. German filling stations are highly competitive and bargains are often available if you shop around, but *not* at autobahn filling stations. Self-service, or *SB-Tanken,* stations are cheapest. Pumps marked *Bleifrei* contain unleaded gas.

ROAD CONDITIONS

Roads in the Berlin and the western part of the country are generally excellent, but some surfaces in eastern Germany, where an urgent improvement program is under way, are in poor condition.

RULES OF THE ROAD

In Germany you drive on the right, and road signs give distances in kilometers. There is no speed limit on autobahns, although drivers are advised to keep below 130 km (80 mi) per hour. Speed limits on non-autobahn country roads vary from 80 to 100 km (50 to 60 mi) per hour. Alcohol limits on drivers are equivalent to two small beers or a quarter of a liter of wine. Note that seat belts must be worn at all times by front- *and* back-seat passengers.

CHILDREN & TRAVEL

CHILDREN IN GERMANY

Most hotels in Germany allow children under a certain age to stay in their parents' room at no extra charge, but others charge them as extra adults; be sure to **ask about the cutoff age for children's discounts.**

➤ BABY-SITTING: For recommended local sitters, **check with your hotel desk.** Updated lists of well-screened baby-sitters are also available from most local tourist offices. Rates are usually about DM 25 per hour. Many large department stores in Germany provide baby-sitting facilities or areas where children can play while their parents shop.

FLYING

If your children are two or older, **ask about children's airfares.** As a general rule, infants under two not occupying a seat fly at greatly reduced fares or even for free.

In general the adult baggage allowance applies to children paying half or more of the adult fare. When booking, **ask about carry-on allowances for those traveling with infants.** In general, for babies charged 10% of the adult fare you are allowed one carry-on bag and a collapsible stroller, which may have to be checked; you may be limited to less if the flight is full.

Experts agree that it's a good idea to use safety seats aloft for children weighing less than 40 pounds. Airlines, however, can set their own policies: U.S. carriers allow FAA-approved models but usually require that you buy a ticket, even if your child would otherwise ride free, since the seats must be strapped into regular seats. Airline rules vary, so it's important to **check your airline's policy about using safety seats during takeoff and landing.** Safety seats cannot obstruct the movement of other passengers in the row, so get an appropriate seat assignment as early as possible.

CONSULATES

Please note: The embassies listed below are branch offices of the embassies' head offices in Bonn. By the year 2000, the United States, among other nations, will have moved their main offices to new facilities in Berlin. Phone numbers and addresses shown below are likely to change in 1999.

➤ ADDRESSES: **Australia** (✉ Uhlandstr. 181–183, ☎ 030/880–0880). **Canada** (✉ International Trade Center, Friedrichstr. 95, ☎ 030/261–1161). **Great Britain** (✉ Unter den Linden 32–34, ☎ 030/201–840). **Ireland** (✉ Ernst-Reuter-Pl. 10, ☎ 030/3480–0822).

United States (✉ Neustädtische Kirchstr. 4–5, ☎ 030/2385–174).

CONSUMER PROTECTION

Whenever possible, **pay with a major credit card** so you can cancel payment or get reimbursed if there's a problem, provided that you can show documentation. This is the best way to pay, whether you're buying travel arrangements before your trip or shopping at your destination.

If you're doing business with a particular company for the first time, **contact your local Better Business Bureau and the attorney general's offices** in your state and the company's home state, as well. Have any complaints been filed?

Finally, if you're buying a package or tour, always **consider travel insurance** that includes default coverage (☞ Insurance, *below*).

➤ LOCAL BBBs: **Council of Better Business Bureaus** (✉ 4200 Wilson Blvd., Suite 800, Arlington, VA 22203, ☎ 703/276–0100, FAX 703/525–8277).

CUSTOMS & DUTIES

When shopping, **keep receipts** for all of your purchases. Upon reentering the country, **be ready to show customs officials what you've bought.** If you feel a duty is incorrect, appeal the assessment. If you object to the way your clearance was handled, get the inspector's badge number. In either case, first ask to see a supervisor, then write to the appropriate authorities, beginning with the port director at your point of entry.

IN GERMANY

Since a single, unrestricted market took effect within the European Union (EU) early in 1993, there are no longer restrictions for citizens of the 15 member countries traveling between EU countries. For instance, travelers may import 800 cigarettes, 120 bottles of wine, and 10 liters of alcohol, provided the goods have been bought duty-paid, i.e., not in a duty-free shop. For citizens of non-EU countries and anyone entering Germany from outside the Union, the following limitations apply.

On goods obtained anywhere outside the EU or for goods purchased in a duty-free shop within an EU country, you are allowed (1) 200 cigarettes or 100 cigarillos or 50 cigars or 250 grams of tobacco (twice that if you live outside of Europe); (2) 2 liters of still table wine; (3) 1 liter of spirits over 22% volume or 2 liters of spirits under 22% volume (fortified and sparkling wines) or 2 more liters of table wine; (4) 60 milliliters of perfume and 250 milliliters of toilet water; (5) other goods to the value of DM 115.

Tobacco and alcohol allowances are for visitors age 17 and over. Other items intended for personal use can be imported and exported freely. There are no restrictions on the import and export of German currency.

IN AUSTRALIA

Australia residents who are 18 or older may bring back $A400 worth of souvenirs and gifts (including jewelry), 250 cigarettes or 250 grams of tobacco, and 1,125 ml of alcohol (including wine, beer, and spirits). Residents under 18 may bring back $A200 worth of goods.

➤ INFORMATION: **Australian Customs Service** (Regional Director, ✉ Box 8, Sydney, NSW 2001, ☎ 02/9213–2000, FAX 02/9213–4000).

IN CANADA

Canadian residents who have been out of Canada for at least seven days may bring in C$500 worth of goods duty-free. If you've been away less than seven days but more than 48 hours, the duty-free allowance drops to C$200; if your trip lasts 24–48 hours, the allowance is C$50. You may not pool allowances with family members. Goods claimed under the C$500 exemption may follow you by mail; those claimed under the lesser exemptions must accompany you. Alcohol and tobacco products may be included in the seven-day and 48-hour exemptions but not in the 24-hour exemption. If you meet the age requirements of the province or territory through which you reenter Canada, you may bring in, duty-free, 1.14 liters (40 imperial ounces) of wine or liquor *or* 24 12-ounce cans or bottles of beer or ale. If you are 16 or older you may bring in, duty-free, 200 cigarettes and 50 cigars.

You may send an unlimited number of gifts worth up to C$60 each duty-free to Canada. Label the package UNSOLICITED GIFT—VALUE UNDER $60. Alcohol and tobacco are excluded.

➤ INFORMATION: **Revenue Canada** (✉ 2265 St. Laurent Blvd. S, Ottawa, Ontario K1G 4K3, ☎ 613/993–0534, 800/461–9999 in Canada).

IN NEW ZEALAND
Homeward-bound residents with goods to declare must present themselves for inspection. If you're 17 or older, you may bring back $700 worth of souvenirs and gifts. Your duty-free allowance also includes 4.5 liters of wine or beer; one 1,125-ml bottle of spirits; and either 200 cigarettes, 250 grams of tobacco, 50 cigars, or a combo of all three up to 250 grams.

➤ INFORMATION: **New Zealand Customs** (✉ Custom House, ✉ 50 Anzac Ave., Box 29, Auckland, New Zealand, ☎ 09/359–6655, ☎ 09/309–2978).

IN THE U.K.
If you are a U.K. resident and your journey was wholly within the European Union (EU), you won't have to pass through customs when you return to the United Kingdom. If you plan to bring back large quantities of alcohol or tobacco, check EU limits beforehand.

➤ INFORMATION: **HM Customs and Excise** (✉ Dorset House, ✉ Stamford St., London SE1 9NG, ☎ 0171/202–4227).

IN THE U.S.
U.S. residents may bring home $400 worth of foreign goods duty-free if they've been out of the country for at least 48 hours (and if they haven't used the $400 allowance or any part of it in the past 30 days).

U.S. residents 21 and older may bring back 1 liter of alcohol duty-free. In addition, regardless of your age, you are allowed 200 cigarettes and 100 non-Cuban cigars. Antiques, which the U.S. Customs Service defines as objects more than 100 years old, enter duty-free, as do original works of art done entirely by hand, including paintings, drawings, and sculptures.

You may also send packages home duty-free: up to $200 worth of goods for personal use, with a limit of one parcel per addressee per day (and no alcohol or tobacco products or perfume worth more than $5); label the package PERSONAL USE, and attach a list of its contents and their retail value. Do not label the package UNSOLICITED

GIFT, or your duty-free exemption will drop to $100. Mailed items do not affect your duty-free allowance on your return.

➤ INFORMATION: **U.S. Customs Service** (Inquiries, ✉ Box 7407, Washington, DC 20044, ☎ 202/927–6724; complaints, Office of Regulations and Rulings, ✉ 1301 Constitution Ave. NW, Washington, DC 20229; registration of equipment, Resource Management, ✉ 1301 Constitution Ave. NW, Washington DC 20229, ☎ 202/927–0540).

DISABILITIES & ACCESSIBILITY

ACCESS IN BERLIN

All major S- and U-bahn stations have elevators, and most buses have hydraulic lifts. Check the public transportation maps or call the **BVG** (Berliner Verkehrsbetriebe, ☎ 030/19449). **Service-Ring-Berlin e.V.** (☎ 030/859–4010) and **Verband Geburts- und anderer Behinderter e.V.** (☎ 030/341–1797) provide information and van and wheelchair rentals.

All the major hotel chains (Hilton, Sheraton, Marriott, Holiday Inn, Steigenberger, and Kempinski) have special facilities for guests with disabilities, including specially equipped and furnished rooms. Some leading privately owned hotels also cater to travelers with disabilities; local tourist offices can provide lists of these hotels and additional information.

MAKING RESERVATIONS

When discussing accessibility with an operator or reservations agent, **ask hard questions.** Are there any stairs, inside *or* out? Are there grab bars next to the toilet *and* in the shower/tub? How wide is the doorway to the room? To the bathroom? For the most extensive facilities meeting the latest legal specifications, **opt for newer accommodations,** which are more likely to have been designed with access in mind. Older buildings or ships may have more limited facilities. Be sure to **discuss your needs before booking.**

TRAVEL AGENCIES & TOUR OPERATORS

As a whole, the travel industry has become more aware of the needs of travelers with disabilities. In the U.S., the Americans with Disabilities Act requires that travel firms serve the needs of all travelers. Note, though, that some agencies and operators specialize in making travel arrangements for individuals and groups with disabilities.

➤ TRAVELERS WITH MOBILITY PROBLEMS: **Access Adventures** (✉ 206 Chestnut Ridge Rd., Rochester, NY 14624, ☎ 716/889–9096), run by a former physical-rehabilitation counselor. **Accessible Journeys** (✉ 35 W. Sellers Ave., Ridley Park, PA 19078, ☎ 610/521–0339 or 800/846–4537, FAX 610/521–6959), for escorted tours exclusively for travelers with mobility impairments. **CareVaca-**

tions (✉ 5019 49th Ave., Suite 102, Leduc, Alberta T9E 6T5, ☎ 403/986–6404, 800/648–1116 in Canada) has group tours and is especially helpful with cruise vacations. **Flying Wheels Travel** (✉ 143 W. Bridge St., Box 382, Owatonna, MN 55060, ☎ 507/451–5005 or 800/535–6790, FAX 507/451–1685), a travel agency specializing in customized tours and itineraries worldwide. **Hinsdale Travel Service** (✉ 201 E. Ogden Ave., Suite 100, Hinsdale, IL 60521, ☎ 630/325–1335), a travel agency that benefits from the advice of wheelchair traveler Janice Perkins.

DISCOUNTS & DEALS

Be a smart shopper and **compare all your options** before making any choice. A plane ticket bought with a promotional coupon may not be cheaper than the least expensive fare from a discount ticket agency. For high-price travel purchases, such as packages or tours, keep in mind that what you get is just as important as what you save. Just because something is cheap doesn't mean it's a bargain.

CLUBS & COUPONS

Many companies sell discounts in the form of travel clubs and coupon books, but these cost money. You must use participating advertisers to get a deal, and only after you recoup the initial membership cost or book price do you begin to save. If you plan to use the club or coupons frequently,

you may save considerably. Before signing up, find out what discounts you get for free.

➤ DISCOUNT CLUBS: **Entertainment Travel Editions** (✉ 2125 Butterfield Rd., Troy, MI 48084, ☎ 800/445–4137; $20–$51, depending on destination). **Great American Traveler** (✉ Box 27965, Salt Lake City, UT 84127, ☎ 801/974–3033 or 800/548–2812; $49.95 per year). **Moment's Notice Discount Travel Club** (✉ 7301 New Utrecht Ave., Brooklyn, NY 11204, ☎ 718/234–6295; $25 per year, single or family). **Privilege Card International** (✉ 237 E. Front St., Youngstown, OH 44503, ☎ 330/746–5211 or 800/236–9732; $74.95 per year). **Sears's Mature Outlook** (✉ Box 9390, Des Moines, IA 50306, ☎ 800/336–6330; $19.95 per year). **Travelers Advantage** (✉ CUC Travel Service, ✉ 3033 S. Parker Rd., Suite 1000, Aurora, CO 80014, ☎ 800/548–1116 or 800/648–4037; $59.95 per year, single or family). **Worldwide Discount Travel Club** (✉ 1674 Meridian Ave., Miami Beach, FL 33139, ☎ 305/534–2082; $50 per year family, $40 single).

CREDIT-CARD BENEFITS

When you use your credit card to make travel purchases you may get free travel-accident insurance, collision-damage insurance, and medical or legal assistance, depending on the card and the bank that issued it. American Express, MasterCard, and Visa provide one or more of these services, so **get a copy of your credit card's travel-benefits policy.** If you are a member of an auto club, always **ask hotel and car-rental reservations agents about auto-club discounts.** Some clubs offer additional discounts on tours, cruises, and admission to attractions.

DISCOUNT RESERVATIONS

To save money, **look into discount-reservations services** with toll-free numbers, which use their buying power to get a better price on hotels, airline tickets, even car rentals. When booking a room, always **call the hotel's local toll-free number** (if one is available) rather than the central reservations number—you'll often get a better price. Always ask about special packages or corporate rates.

When shopping for the best deal on hotels and car rentals, **look for guaranteed exchange rates,** which protect you against a falling dollar. With your rate locked in, you won't pay more, even if the price goes up in the local currency.

➤ AIRLINE TICKETS: ☎ **800/FLY–4–LESS.**

➤ HOTEL ROOMS: **Hotels Plus** (☎ 800/235–0909). **International Marketing & Travel Concepts** (☎ 800/790–4682). **Steigenberger Reservation Service** (☎ 800/223–5652). **Travel Interlink** (☎ 800/888–5898).

PACKAGE DEALS

Packages and guided tours can save you money, but don't confuse the two. When you buy a package, your travel remains independent, just as though you had planned and booked the trip yourself. Fly/drive packages, which combine airfare and car rental, are often a good deal.

ELECTRICITY

To use your U.S.-purchased electric-powered equipment, **bring a converter and adapter.** The electrical current in Germany is 220 volts, 50 cycles alternating current (AC); wall outlets take continental-type plugs, with two round prongs.

If your appliances are dual-voltage, you'll need only an adapter. Don't use 110-volt outlets, marked FOR SHAVERS ONLY, for high-wattage appliances such as blow-dryers. Most laptops operate equally well on 110 and 220 volts and so require only an adapter.

EMERGENCIES

Police (☎ 030/110).

Ambulance (☎ 030/112).

Ambulance and emergency medical attention (☎ 030/310–031).

Dentist (☎ 030/8900–4333).

LATE-NIGHT PHARMACIES

Pharmacies in Berlin offer late-night service on a rotating basis. Every pharmacy displays a notice indicating the location of the nearest shop with evening hours. For **emergency pharmaceutical assistance,** call ☎ 030/01141.

GAY & LESBIAN TRAVEL

➤ GAY- AND LESBIAN-FRIENDLY TRAVEL AGENCIES: **Corniche Travel** (⊠ 8721 Sunset Blvd., Suite 200, West Hollywood, CA 90069, ☎ 310/854–6000 or 800/429–8747, ℻ 310/659–7441). **Islanders Kennedy Travel** (⊠ 183 W. 10th St., New York, NY 10014, ☎ 212/242–3222 or 800/988–1181, ℻ 212/929–8530). **Now Voyager** (⊠ 4406 18th St., San Francisco, CA 94114, ☎ 415/626–1169 or 800/255–6951, ℻ 415/626–8626). **Yellowbrick Road** (⊠ 1500 W. Balmoral Ave., Chicago, IL 60640, ☎ 773/561–1800 or 800/642–2488, ℻ 773/561–4497). **Skylink Travel and Tour** (⊠ 3577 Moorland Ave., Santa Rosa, CA 95407, ☎ 707/585–8355 or 800/225–5759, ℻ 707/584–5637), serving lesbian travelers.

GUIDED TOURS

BOAT TRIPS

Tours of downtown Berlin's **canals** take in sights such as the Charlottenburg Palace and the Congress Hall. Tours depart from Kottbusser Bridge in Kreuzberg and cost around DM 10.

A tour of the **Havel Lakes** is the thing to do in summer. Trips begin at Wannsee (S-bahn: Wannsee) and at the Greenwich Promenade in Tegel (U-bahn: Tegel). You'll sail on either the whale-shaped vessel *Moby Dick* or the *Havel Queen*, a Mississippi-style boat, and cruise 28 km (17 mi) through the lakes and past forests. Tours last 4½ hours and cost between DM 15 and DM 20. There are 20 operators.

➤ HAVEL LAKES TOURS: **Reederei Bruno Winkler** (⊠ Mierendorffstr. 16, ☎ 030/3499–595). **Reederei Heinz Riedel** (⊠ Planufer 78, ☎ 030/693–4646). **Stern- und Kreisschiffahrt** (⊠ Puschkinallee 16-17, ☎ 030/5363–600).

BUS TOURS

Four companies offer more or less identical tours (in English) covering all major sights in Berlin, as well as all-day tours to Potsdam, Dresden, and Meissen. The Berlin tours cost DM 25–DM 45; those to Potsdam, DM 50–DM 70; and to Dresden and Meissen, approximately DM 100.

➤ BUS TOURS: **Berliner Bären Stadtrundfahrten** (BBS, ⊠ Seeburgerstr. 19b, ☎ 030/3519–5270). Groups depart from the corner of Rankestrasse and Kurfürstendamm and in eastern Berlin, from Alexanderplatz, in front of the Forum Hotel. **Berolina Stadtrundfahrten** (⊠ Kurfürstendamm 22, corner Meinekestr., ☎ 030/8856–8030). Groups depart from the corner of Kurfürstendamm and Meinekestrasse and in eastern Berlin, from Alexanderplatz, in front of the Forum Hotel. **Bus**

Verkehr Berlin (BVB, ⊠ Kurfürstendamm 225, ☎ 030/885–9880). Tours leave from Kurfürstendamm 225. **Severin & Kühn** (⊠ Kurfürstendamm 216, ☎ 030/8804–190). Groups leave from clearly marked stops along the Kurfürstendamm and in eastern Berlin, at the corner of Unter den Linden and Friedrichstrasse.

SPECIAL-INTEREST TOURS

Sightseeing tours with a cultural/historical focus are offered weekends at a cost of approximately DM 15 by **StattReisen** (⊠ Malplaquetstr. 5, ☎ 030/455–3028). Tours include "Jewish History" and "Prenzlauer Berg Neighborhoods" and are in German; English tours are offered upon request. All tours given by **Berlin Walks** (⊠ Habigstr. 26, ☎ 030/3019–194) are in English. The introductory "Discover Berlin" tour takes in the major downtown sites in 2½ to 3 hours. Other theme tours (Infamous Third Reich Sites and Jewish Life in Berlin) are shorter and run April–December. Tours depart at the taxi stand in front of the main entrance to the Zoologischer Garten train station and cost DM 15, plus S-bahn transportation.

HEALTH

MEDICAL PLANS

No one plans to get sick while traveling, but it happens, so **consider signing up with a medical-assistance company.** Members get doctor referrals, emergency evacuation or repatriation, 24-hour telephone hotlines for medical consultation, cash for emergencies, and other personal and legal assistance. Coverage varies by plan, so **review the benefits of each carefully.**

➤ MEDICAL-ASSISTANCE COMPANIES: **International SOS Assistance** (⊠ 8 Neshaminy Interplex, Suite 207, Trevose, PA 19053, ☎ 215/245–4707 or 800/523–6586, FAX 215/244–9617; ⊠ 12 Chemin Riantbosson, 1217 Meyrin 1, Geneva, Switzerland, ☎ 4122/785–6464, FAX 4122/785–6424; ⊠ 10 Anson Rd., 14-07/08 International Plaza, Singapore, 079903, ☎ 65/226–3936, FAX 65/226–3937).

HOLIDAYS

The following national holidays are observed in Germany: January 1; April 2 (Good Friday); April 5 (Easter Monday); May 1 (Workers' Day); May 13 (Ascension); May 24 (Pentecost Monday); October 3 (German Unity Day); November 1 (All Saints' Day); December 24–26 (Christmas).

INSURANCE

Travel insurance is the best way to **protect yourself against financial loss.** The most useful plan is a comprehensive policy that includes coverage for trip cancellation and interruption, default, trip delay, and medical expenses (with a waiver for preexisting conditions).

Without insurance, you will lose all or most of your money if you cancel your trip, regardless of the reason. Default insurance covers you if your tour operator, airline, or cruise line goes out of business. Trip-delay covers unforeseen expenses that you may incur due to bad weather or mechanical delays. It's important to compare the fine print regarding trip-delay coverage when comparing policies.

For overseas travel, one of the most important components of travel insurance is its medical coverage. Supplemental health insurance will pick up the cost of your medical bills should you get sick or injured while traveling. U.S. residents should note that Medicare generally does not cover health-care costs outside the United States, nor do many privately issued policies. Residents of the United Kingdom can buy an annual travel-insurance policy valid for most vacations taken during the year in which the coverage is purchased. If you are pregnant or have a preexisting condition, make sure you're covered. British citizens should buy extra medical coverage when traveling overseas, according to the Association of British Insurers. Australian travelers should buy travel insurance, including extra medical coverage, whenever they go abroad, according to the Insurance Council of Australia.

Always **buy travel insurance directly from the insurance company**; if you buy it from a cruise line, airline, or tour operator that goes out of business you probably will not be covered for the agency or operator's default. Before you make any purchase, **review your existing health and home-owner's policies** to find out whether they cover expenses incurred while traveling.

➤ TRAVEL INSURERS: In the U.S., **Access America** (✉ 6600 W. Broad St., Richmond, VA 23230, ☎ 804/285–3300 or 800/284–8300). **Travel Guard International** (✉ 1145 Clark St., Stevens Point, WI 54481, ☎ 715/345–0505 or 800/826–1300). In Canada, **Mutual of Omaha** (✉ Travel Division, ✉ 500 University Ave., Toronto, Ontario M5G 1V8, ☎ 416/598–4083, 800/268–8825 in Canada).

➤ INSURANCE INFORMATION: In the U.K., **Association of British Insurers** (✉ 51 Gresham St., London EC2V 7HQ, ☎ 0171/600–3333). In Australia, the **Insurance Council of Australia** (☎ 613/9614–1077, ⅀ 613/9614–7924).

LANGUAGE

Germans make fun of the harsh Berlin accent, but it is hardly the heavy dialect of Bavaria.

The Germans are great linguists and you'll find that English is spoken in virtually all hotels, restaurants, airports, stations, museums, and other places of interest.

Berliners who hail from the former West Germany will most likely have had English classes in school; Berliners from the former East Germany are less likely to be familiar with English.

Berliners appreciated John F. Kennedy's attempt to express his unity with them in German. In a public gathering near the then newly built wall, President Kennedy claimed, "Ich bin ein Berliner." While it was understood that he meant, "I am a Berliner," his words actually meant, "I am a jelly doughnut." (A Berliner is the term for a particular pastry in Berlin.)

LODGING

The standard of German hotels is very high. Rates vary enormously, though not disproportionately, in comparison with other northern European countries. You can nearly always **expect courteous and polite service and clean and comfortable rooms.** Larger hotels often have no-smoking rooms or even no-smoking floors, so it's always worth asking for one when you check in.

Lists of German hotels are available from the German National Tourist Office and all regional and local tourist offices. (Most hotels have restaurants, but those listed as *Garni* will provide breakfast only.) Tourist offices will also make bookings for you at a nominal fee, but they may have difficulty doing

so after 4 PM in high season and on weekends, so **don't wait until too late in the day to begin looking for your accommodations.**

HOSTELS

No matter what your age, you can **save on lodging costs by staying at hostels.** In some 5,000 locations in more than 70 countries around the world, Hostelling International (HI), the umbrella group for a number of national youth hostel associations, offers single-sex, dorm-style beds and, at many hostels, "couples" rooms and family accommodations. Membership in any HI national hostel association, open to travelers of all ages, allows you to stay in HI-affiliated hostels at member rates (one-year membership is about $25 for adults; hostels run about $10–$25 per night). Members also have priority if the hostel is full; they're eligible for discounts around the world, even on rail and bus travel in some countries.

➤ HOSTEL ORGANIZATIONS: **Hostelling International—American Youth Hostels** (✉ 733 15th St. NW, Suite 840, Washington, DC 20005, ☎ 202/783–6161, FAX 202/783–6171). **Hostelling International—Canada** (✉ 400-205 Catherine St., Ottawa, Ontario K2P 1C3, ☎ 613/237–7884, FAX 613/237–7868). **Youth Hostel Association of England and Wales** (✉ Trevelyan House, 8 St. Stephen's Hill, St. Albans, Hertfordshire AL1 2DY, ☎ 01727/

855215 or 01727/845047, ⒻⒶⓍ 01727/844126); membership in the U.S. $25, in Canada C$26.75, in the U.K. £9.30).

➤ IN GERMANY: **Deutsches Jugendherbergswerk Hauptverband** (✉ Postfach 1455, D–32704 Detmold, ☎ 05231/74010) has listings of German youth hostels.

MAIL

POSTAL RATES
Airmail letters to the United States and Canada cost DM 3; postcards cost DM 2. All letters to the United Kingdom cost DM 1.10; postcards cost DM 1.

RECEIVING MAIL
You can arrange to have mail sent to you in care of any German post office; **have the envelope marked "Postlagernd."** This service is free. Alternatively, have mail sent to an American Express office. There's no charge to cardholders, holders of American Express traveler's checks, or anyone who has booked a vacation with American Express.

MONEY

CREDIT & DEBIT CARDS
Should you use a credit card or a debit card when traveling? Both have benefits. A credit card allows you to delay payment and gives you certain rights as a consumer (☞ Consumer Protection, *above*). A debit card, also known as a check card, deducts funds directly from your checking account and helps you stay within your budget.

If you want to rent a car, though, you may still need an old-fashioned credit card. Although you can always *pay* for your car with a debit card, some agencies will not allow you to *reserve* a car with a debit card.

Otherwise, the two types of plastic are virtually the same. Both will get you cash advances at ATMs worldwide if your card is properly programmed with your personal identification number (PIN). (For use in Germany, your PIN must be four digits long.) Both offer excellent, wholesale exchange rates. And both protect you against unauthorized use if the card is lost or stolen. Your liability is limited to $50, as long as you report the card missing.

➤ ATM LOCATIONS: **Cirrus** (☎ 800/424–7787). **Plus** (☎ 800/843–7587) for locations in the U.S. and Canada, or visit your local bank.

CURRENCY
The European Union currency unit, the Euro, makes its official appearance on January 1, 1999, although it will take two years for the complete introduction of the new banknotes and coins. Deutschmarks will still be the official currency for everyday use in 1999, although some shops might begin to price their wares in Euros. Don't let that confuse you, and continue to think in terms of Deutschmarks—at least until the year 2002, when full currency union takes effect. The

Deutschmark (DM) is divided into 100 pfennigs (pf). There are bills of 5 (rare), 10, 20, 50, 100, 200, 500, and 1,000 marks and coins of 1, 2, 5, 10, and 50 pfennigs and 1, 2, and 5 marks. At press time, the mark stood at DM 1.79 to the U.S. dollar, DM 1.20 to the Canadian dollar, and DM 2.98 to the pound sterling.

EXCHANGING MONEY

For the most favorable rates, **change money through banks.** Although fees charged for ATM transactions may be higher abroad than at home, Cirrus and Plus exchange rates are excellent, because they are based on wholesale rates offered only by major banks. You won't do as well at exchange booths in airports or rail and bus stations, in hotels, in restaurants, or in stores, although you may find their hours more convenient. To avoid lines at airport exchange booths, **get a bit of local currency before you leave home.**

➤ EXCHANGE SERVICES: **Chase *Currency To Go*** (☎ 800/935–9935; 935–9935 in NY, NJ, and CT). **International Currency Express** (☎ 888/842–0880 on the East Coast, 888/278–6628 on the West Coast). **Thomas Cook Currency Services** (☎ 800/287–7362 for telephone orders and retail locations).

PACKING

LUGGAGE

How many carry-on bags you can bring with you is up to the airline. Most allow two, but on certain flights the limit is often reduced to one. Gate agents will take excess baggage—including bags they deem oversize—from you as you board and add it to checked luggage. To avoid this situation, make sure that everything you carry aboard will fit under your seat.

If you are flying internationally, note that baggage allowances may be determined not by piece but by weight—generally 88 pounds (40 kilograms) in first class, 66 pounds (30 kilograms) in business class, and 44 pounds (20 kilograms) in economy.

Airline liability for baggage is limited to $1,250 per person on flights within the United States. On international flights it amounts to $9.07 per pound or $20 per kilogram for checked baggage (roughly $640 per 70-pound bag) and $400 per passenger for unchecked baggage. You can buy additional coverage at check-in for about $10 per $1,000 of coverage, but it excludes a rather extensive list of items, shown on your airline ticket.

Before departure, **itemize your bags' contents** and their worth, and label the bags with your name, address, and phone number. (If you use your home address, cover it so that potential thieves can't see it readily.) Inside each bag, **pack a copy of your itinerary. At check-in, make sure that each**

bag is correctly tagged with the destination airport's three-letter code. If your bags arrive damaged or fail to arrive at all, file a written report with the airline before leaving the airport.

PACKING LIST

What you pack depends more on the time of year than on any particular dress code. Winters can be bitterly cold; summers are warm but with days that suddenly turn cool and rainy so **take a warm sweater and rain-repellent jacket.**

Jeans are as popular in Germany as anywhere else and are perfectly acceptable for sightseeing and informal dining. In the evening, men will probably feel more comfortable wearing a jacket and tie in more expensive restaurants, although it is almost never required. Many German women are extremely fashion-conscious and wear stylish outfits to restaurants and the theater, especially in the larger cities.

To discourage purse snatchers and pickpockets, **carry a handbag with long straps** that you can sling across your body, bandolier-style, and a zippered compartment for money and other valuables.

For stays in budget hotels, **take your own soap and washcloth.** Many provide no soap at all or only one small bar.

In your carry-on luggage **bring an extra pair of eyeglasses or contact lenses** and **enough of any medication you take** to last the entire trip. You may also want your doctor to write a spare prescription using the drug's generic name, since brand names may vary from country to country. **Never put prescription drugs or valuables in luggage to be checked.** To avoid customs delays, carry medications in their original packaging. And don't forget to copy down and carry addresses of offices that handle refunds of lost traveler's checks.

PASSPORTS

When traveling internationally, **carry a passport even if you don't need one** (it's always the best form of I.D.), and make **two photocopies of the data page** (one for someone at home and another for you, carried separately from your passport). If you lose your passport, promptly call the nearest embassy or consulate and the local police.

ENTERING GERMANY

U.S., Canadian, and British citizens need only a valid passport to enter Germany for stays of up to 90 days.

PASSPORT OFFICES

The best time to apply for a passport or to renew is during the fall and winter. Before any trip, be sure to check your passport's expiration date and, if necessary, renew it as soon as possible. (Some countries won't allow you to enter on a passport that's due to expire in six months or less.)

➤ AUSTRALIAN CITIZENS: **Australian Passport Office** (☎ 131–232).

➤ CANADIAN CITIZENS: **Passport Office** (☎ 819/994–3500 or 800/567–6868).

➤ NEW ZEALAND CITIZENS: **New Zealand Passport Office** (☎ 04/494–0700 for information on how to apply, 0800/727–776 for information on applications already submitted).

➤ U.K. CITIZENS: **London Passport Office** (☎ 0990/21010), for fees and documentation requirements and to request an emergency passport.

➤ U.S. CITIZENS: **National Passport Information Center** (☎ 900/225–5674; calls are charged at 35¢ per minute for automated service, $1.05 per minute for operator service).

SENIOR-CITIZEN TRAVEL

In Germany, the number of citizens over 60 is growing; this section of the population has also become more affluent and even has its own political party, the Gray Panthers. The strength of this special-interest age group has won them special privileges in Germany—such as price adjustments on the railways and reduced admission to museums—and elderly visitors from abroad can also take advantage of these discounts. Contact the German National Tourist Office (☞ Visitor Information, *below*).

To qualify for age-related discounts, **mention your senior-citizen status up front** when booking hotel reservations (not when checking out) and before you're seated in restaurants (not when paying the bill). Note that discounts may be limited to certain menus, days, or hours. When renting a car, **ask about promotional car-rental discounts,** which can be cheaper than senior-citizen rates.

➤ EDUCATIONAL PROGRAMS: **Elderhostel** (✉ 75 Federal St., 3rd floor, Boston, MA 02110, ☎ 617/426–8056). **Interhostel** (✉ University of New Hampshire, 6 Garrison Ave., Durham, NH 03824, ☎ 603/862–1147 or 800/733–9753, FAX 603/862–1113).

STUDENT TRAVEL

HOSTELING

Germany's youth hostels—*Jugendherbergen* —are probably the most efficient, up-to-date, and proportionally numerous of any country's. Since unification, many eastern German youth hostels have closed down. An effort is being made, however, to keep as many open as possible, and renovations are currently under way to bring eastern hostels up to the standards of their western counterparts.

There are no restrictions on age in Berlin, though those under 20 get preference when space is limited.

Preference is also given to members of a national youth hosteling or Hostelling International (HI); non-members pay an extra DM 6–DM 7 for the first six nights' accommodation, after which normal hostel charges are levied. These range from about DM 15 to DM 21 for young people under 27 and DM 25–DM 38 for those 27 and older (breakfast included). Cards are available from the American Youth Hostels Association, the Canadian Hostelling Association, and the United Kingdom's Youth Hostels Association (☞ Lodging, *above*).

TRAVEL AGENCIES

To save money, **look into deals available through student-oriented travel agencies.** To qualify you'll need a bona fide student I.D. card. Members of international student groups are also eligible.

➤ STUDENT I.D.S & SERVICES: **Council on International Educational Exchange** (⊠ CIEE, 205 E. 42nd St., 14th floor, New York, NY 10017, ☎ 212/822–2600 or 888/268–6245, FAX 212/822–2699), for mail orders only, in the United States. **Travel Cuts** (⊠ 187 College St., Toronto, Ontario M5T 1P7, ☎ 416/979–2406 or 800/667–2887) in Canada.

TELEPHONES

COUNTRY CODES

The country code for Germany is 49. When dialing a German number from abroad, drop the initial 0 from the local area code.

DIRECTORY & OPERATOR INFORMATION

The German telephone system is fully automatic, and it's unlikely that you'll have to employ the services of an operator, unless you're seeking information. If you have difficulty reaching your number or want to book a reverse-charge call, dial 010, or 0010 for international calls. For information, dial 11833. International operators speak English, and English-speaking staff are close at hand for other services.

INTERNATIONAL CALLS

International calls can be made from public phones bearing the sign INLANDS UND AUSLANDSGE-SPRÄCHE. Using DM 5 coins is best for long-distance dialing; a four-minute call to the United States costs DM 15. To avoid weighing yourself down with coins, however, use a phone card or **make international calls from post offices**; even those in small country towns will have a special booth for international calls. You pay the clerk the cost of the call, plus a DM 2 connection fee. Never make international calls from your hotel room; rates will be at least double the regular charge.

AT&T, MCI, and Sprint international access codes make calling the United States relatively convenient, but you may find the local access number blocked in many hotel rooms. First ask the hotel operator to connect you. If the hotel operator balks, ask for an international operator, or dial the international operator yourself. One way to improve your odds of getting connected to your long-distance carrier is to travel with more than one company's calling card (a hotel may block Sprint, for example, but not MCI). If all else fails, call from a pay phone in the hotel lobby.

➤ ACCESS CODES: **AT&T Direct** (☎ 800/435–0812). **MCI World-Phone** (☎ 800/444–4141). **Sprint International Access** (☎ 800/877–4646).

PUBLIC PHONES

Local public phones charge a minimum 30 pfennigs per call (for six minutes). All public phones take 10 pf, DM 1, and DM 5 coins, although coin-operated call boxes are rapidly giving way to card-operated ones. So you're advised to **buy a phone card,** particularly if you're anticipating making a lot of phone calls. You can purchase a phone card at any German post office (also available at many exchange places). They come in denominations of DM 12 and DM 50, the latter good for DM 60 worth of calls. Most phone booths have instructions in English as well as German.

TIPPING

The service charges on bills suffice for most tips in your hotel, though you should **tip bellhops and porters**; DM 2 per bag or service is ample. It's also customary to leave a small tip (a couple of marks per

night) for the room cleaning staff. Whether you tip the desk clerk depends on whether he or she has given you any special service.

Service charges are included in all restaurant checks (listed as *Bedienung*), as is tax (listed as *MWST*). Nonetheless, it is customary to **round up the bill to the nearest mark or to leave about 5%** (give it to the waiter or waitress as you pay the bill; don't leave it on the table).

In taxis, **round up the fare to the nearest full mark** as a tip. Only give more if you have particularly cumbersome or heavy luggage (though you will be charged 50 pfennigs for each piece of luggage anyway).

TOUR OPERATORS

Buying a prepackaged tour or independent vacation can make your trip to Germany less expensive and more hassle-free. Because everything is prearranged, you'll spend less time planning.

Operators that handle several hundred thousand travelers per year can use their purchasing power to give you a good price. Their high volume may also indicate financial stability. But some small companies provide more personalized service; because they tend to specialize, they may also be more knowledgeable about a given area.

BOOKING WITH AN AGENT

Travel agents are excellent resources. In fact, large operators accept bookings made only through travel agents. But it's a good idea to **collect brochures from several agencies,** because some agents' suggestions may be influenced by relationships with tour and package firms that reward them for volume sales. If you have a special interest, **find an agent with expertise in that area;** ASTA (☞ Travel Agencies, *below*) has a database of specialists worldwide.

Make sure your travel agent knows the accommodations and other services. You may want to ask about the hotel's location, room size, beds, and whether it has a pool, room service, or programs for children. Has your agent been there in person or sent others you can contact?

Do some homework on your own, too: Local tourism boards can provide information about lesser-known and small-niche operators, some of which may sell only direct.

BUYER BEWARE

Each year consumers are stranded or lose their money when tour operators—even very large ones with excellent reputations—go out of business. So **check out the operator.** Find out how long the company has been in business, and ask several travel agents about its reputation. If the package or tour you are considering is priced lower than in your wildest dreams, **be skeptical.** Try to **book with a company that has a consumer-protec-** **tion program.** If the operator has such a program, you'll find information about it in the company's brochure. If the operator you are considering does not offer some kind of consumer protection, then ask for references from satisfied customers.

In the U.S., members of the National Tour Association and United States Tour Operators Association are required to set aside funds to cover your payments and travel arrangements in case the company defaults. It's also a good idea to choose a company that participates in the American Society of Travel Agents' Tour Operator Program (TOP). This gives you a forum if there are any disputes between you and your tour operator; ASTA will act as mediator.

➤ TOUR-OPERATOR RECOMMENDATIONS: **American Society of Travel Agents** (☞ Travel Agencies, *below*). **National Tour Association** (✉ NTA, 546 E. Main St., Lexington, KY 40508, ☎ 606/226–4444 or 800/755–8687). **United States Tour Operators Association** (✉ USTOA, 342 Madison Ave., Suite 1522, New York, NY 10173, ☎ 212/599–6599 or 800/468–7862, ℻ 212/599–6744).

PACKAGES

Like group tours, independent vacation packages are available from major tour operators and airlines. The companies listed below offer vacation packages in a broad price range.

➤ AIR/HOTEL: **Delta Vacations**
(☎ 800/872–7786). **DER Tours**
(✉ 9501 W. Devon St., Rosemont,
IL 60018, ☎ 800/937–1235, FAX
847/692–4141 or 800/282–7474,
800/860–9944 for brochures).
TWA Getaway Vacations
(☞ Group Tours, *above*).

➤ FROM THE U.K.: **DER Travel
Services Ltd.** (✉ 18 Conduit St.,
London W1R 9TD, ☎ 0171/290–
0111) arranges self-catering,
guest-house, and hotel vacations.
The **German Travel Centre** (✉
403–409 Rayner's La., Pinner,
Middlesex, HA5 5ER, ☎ 0181/
429–2900) arranges tailor-made
vacations. **Moswin Tours Ltd.**
(✉ 21 Church St., Oadby, Leices-
ter LE2 5DB, ☎ 0116/271–9922)
specializes in spa resorts and city
breaks in Germany.

TRANSPORTATION

BIKE

Bicycling is popular in Berlin; not
only does it help in getting a sense
of how the city is laid out, but it's
also a quick way to navigate between the central tourist areas. Although biking is not recommended
in the heavily traveled areas downtown, you'll see plenty of helmet-
less locals braving the traffic or
carrying along their bikes in the
subways. Biking is ideal in outlying neighborhoods and in the large
parks. Bike paths are generally
marked by red bricks on the walk-
ways; many stores that rent or sell
bikes carry the Berlin biker's atlas
to help you find the paths. See Bik-

ing *in* Chapter 6 for more information about where to rent bikes.

BUS AND SUBWAY

Berlin is too large to be explored
on foot. To compensate, the city
has one of the most efficient public-transportation systems in Europe, a smoothly integrated
network of subway (U-bahn) and
suburban (S-bahn) train lines,
buses, trams (in eastern Berlin
only), and even a ferry across the
Wannsee Lake, making every part
of the city easily accessible. Extensive all-night bus and tram service
operates seven nights a weeks (in-
dicated by the letter N next to
route numbers).

A DM 3.90 ticket covers not only
the downtown areas (fare zones A
and B), but the outlying areas
(fare zone C) as well, for two
hours and allows you to make an
unlimited number of changes between trains, buses, and trams.

If you are just making a short trip,
buy a **Kurzstreckentarif.** It allows
you to ride six bus stops or three
U-bahn or S-bahn stops for DM
2.50. The best deal for visitors
who plan to travel around the city
extensively is the **day card** for DM
7.50, valid until 3 AM of the following day after validation. It's
good for all trains and buses. The
group day card, DM 20, offers the
same benefits as the day card for
two adults and up to three children. A seven-day **tourist pass**
costs DM 40 and allows unlimited
travel on all city buses and trains

for fare zones A and B; DM 45 buys all three fare zones. The **Berlin WelcomeCard** costs DM 16 (for one person) and entitles one adult and up to three children to two days (DM 29) of unlimited travel as well as free admission or reductions of up to 50% for sightseeing trips, museums, theaters, and other events and attractions.

All tickets are available from vending machines at U-bahn and S-bahn stations. Punch your ticket into the red machine on the platform. For information about public transportation, call the **Berliner Verkehrsbetriebe** (☎ 030/19449) or go to the BVG-information office on Hardenbergplatz, directly in front of the Bahnhof Zoo train station. If you're caught without a ticket, the fine is DM 60.

Please note: Subway fares quoted above were the ones available at press time (summer 1998). Fares and ticket regulations will likely be different in 1999.

LONG-DISTANCE BUS SERVICE

Buses are slightly cheaper than trains. Berlin is linked by bus to 170 European cities. The Ombinusbahnhof, the central bus terminal, is at the corner of Masurenallee 4–6 and Messedamm. Reserve through DER (state agency), commercial travel agencies, or the station itself. For information, call ☎ 030/301–8028 between 9 and 5:30.

TAXIS

The base rate is DM 4, after which prices vary according to a complex tariff system. Figure on paying around DM 15 for a ride the length of Ku'damm. Ask for a special fare called *Kurzstreckentarif,* which allows for a short ride of less than 2 km (1 mi) or five minutes in a hailed cab in the street only. You can also hail one at a taxi stand or order a cab by calling 030/9644, 030/210–202, 030/691–001, or 030/261–026. U-bahn employees will call a taxi for passengers after 8 PM.

A new service offered in the downtown areas is *Velotaxis,* a rickshaw service system operated by students along Kurfürstendamm and Unter den Linden. Just hail one of the orange or red bicycle cabs on the street or look for the velotaxi stand signs along the boulevards mentioned. The fare is DM 2 (for up to 1 km/⅔ mi), DM 5 for a tour between sightseeing landmarks (for example, Europa Center to the Brandenburger Tor), and DM 15 for 30 minutes of individual travel. Velotaxis operate April–October, 1 PM–8 PM only. For more information call 030/4435–8990.

TRAIN

There are six major rail routes to Berlin from the western part of the country (from Hamburg, Hannover, Köln, Frankfurt, Munich, and Nürnberg), and the rail network in the east has expanded considerably, making all of eastern Germany more accessible. Service between Berlin and eastern Europe has also improved significantly, resulting in shorter traveling times. Ask about reduced fares within Germany; three people or more can often travel at discounted rates. Some trains now stop at and depart from more than one of Berlin's four main train stations, but generally west- and north-originating trains arrive at Friedrichstrasse and Zoologischer Garten, and east- and south-originating trains at Hauptbahnhof and Lichtenberg. For details on rates and information, call **Deutsche Bahn Information** (☎ 030/19419).

TRAVEL AGENCIES

A good travel agent puts your needs first. Look for an agency that has been in business at least five years, emphasizes customer service, and has someone on staff who specializes in your destination. In addition, **make sure the agency belongs to a professional trade organization,** such as ASTA in the United States. If your travel agency is also acting as your tour operator, *see* Buyer Beware in Tour Operators, *above*.

➤ LOCAL AGENT REFERRALS: **American Society of Travel Agents** (ASTA, ☎ 800/965–2782 24-hr hotline, FAX 703/684–8319). **Association of Canadian Travel Agents** (⊠ 1729 Bank St., Suite 201, Ot-tawa, Ontario K1V 7Z5, ☎ 613/521–0474, FAX 613/521–0805). **Association of British Travel Agents** (⊠ 55–57 Newman St., London W1P 4AH, ☎ 0171/637–2444, FAX 0171/637–0713). **Australian Federation of Travel Agents** (☎ 02/9264–3299). **Travel Agents' Association of New Zealand** (☎ 04/499–0104).

➤ WITHIN BERLIN: **American Express Reisebüro** (⊠ at Wittenbgerpl., Bayreuther Str. 37, ☎ 030/2149–8363; ⊠ Uhlandstr. 173, ☎ 030/882–7575; ⊠ Friedrichstr. 172, ☎ 030/238–4102). **American Lloyd** (⊠ Kurfürstendamm 209, ☎ 030/20740).

U.S. GOVERNMENT

Government agencies can be an excellent source of inexpensive travel information. When planning your trip, **find out what government materials are available.**

➤ ADVISORIES: **U.S. Department of State** (⊠ Overseas Citizens Services Office, Room 4811 N.S., Washington, DC 20520; ☎ 202/647–5225 or FAX 202/647–3000 for interactive hotline; ☎ 301/946–4400 for computer bulletin board); enclose a self-addressed, stamped, business-size envelope.

➤ PAMPHLETS: **Consumer Information Center** (⊠ Consumer Information Catalogue, Pueblo, CO 81009, ☎ 719/948–3334 or 888/878–3256) for a free catalog that includes travel titles.

VISITOR INFORMATION

In addition to through the offices listed below, detailed information about what's going on in Berlin can be found in the German-language *Berlin Programm,* a monthly tourist guide to Berlin arts, museums, and theaters; and the magazines *Prinz, tip,* and *zitty,* which appear every two weeks and provide full arts listings. The only English-language magazine available is the tourist office's *Berlin–the magazine* (DM 3.50), published four times a year.

A **Berlin Hotline** provides the latest tourist information via phone (☎ 030/250–025) or fax (FAX 030/2500–2424).

➤ BERLIN TOURIST OFFICE: For materials on the city before your trip, write **Berlin Tourismus Marketing GmbH** (✉ Am Karlsbad 11, D-10785 Berlin). For information on the spot, the main office at the back of the Europa Center (✉ Budapester Strasse,) is open Monday–Saturday 8 AM–10 PM, Sunday 9–9. Other offices are found at the Brandenburger Tor (✉ Pariser Platz), open Monday–Saturday 9:30–6; and at the Tegel Airport, open daily 5 AM–10:30 PM.

➤ FOR WOMEN: **Fraueninfothek Berlin** (✉ Dircksenstr. 47, ☎ 030/ 283–2737) is an information center for women that helps find accommodations and gives information on upcoming events. It's open Tuesday–Saturday 9–9, Sunday and holidays 9–3.

➤ GERMAN NATIONAL TOURIST OFFICE: **U.S. Nationwide:** (✉ 122 E. 42nd St., New York, NY 10168, ☎ 212/661–7200, FAX 212/661–7174). **Canada:** (✉ 175 Bloor St. E, Suite 604, Toronto, Ontario M4W 3R8, ☎ 416/968–1570, FAX 416/968–1986). **U.K.:** (✉ Nightingale House, 65 Curzon St., London W1Y 8NE, ☎ 0171/493–0081 or 0891/600–100 for brochures, FAX 0171/495–6129). Calls to the brochure line cost 50p per minute peak rate, 45p at all other times.

WEATHER

Berlin's climate is temperate, although cold spells, rainy weather, and many overcast days can make temperate seem a lot worse than it sounds. Summers can be sunny and warm, though you should **be prepared for a few cloudy and wet days.** Germans measure temperature Celsius, not Fahrenheit. Multiply the Celsius temperature by 1.8 and add 32 to get the Fahrenheit equivalent. For example, 23.9 °C is a beautiful day of 75 °F; 10 °C is a chilly 50 °F.

1 Destination: Berlin

BERLIN ON THE CUTTING EDGE

AS THE 20TH CENTURY draws to an end, Berlin, a metropolis born again, is heading for a bright future. Berlin's role as the focal point and touchstone of a reuniting Germany began on November 9, 1989, when the infamous Berlin Wall fell, and culminated two years later in the historic parliamentary vote to make the city once again the seat of the federal government and the parliament. Thus the end of the cold war was signaled in the city that was both the beginning cause and the trapped victim of one of the greatest geographic and political anomalies of all time. For nearly 30 years Berlin was split in two by a concrete wall more than 12 ft high—its larger western half an island of capitalist democracy surrounded by an East Germany run by hard-line Communists. Built in 1961 at the height of the cold war, the Berlin Wall symbolized the separation of two sharply different political and economic systems. Ironically, though, it also became a major tourist attraction, where viewing platforms along the western side enabled visitors to see the battlefrontlike no-man's-land on the other side, guarded by soldiers and peppered with booby traps. The wall's demolition cast it once more as a symbol—this time of the change sweeping over former Iron Curtain countries. With the wall gone, and mostly recycled into street gravel, only four large chunks remain as reminders of the grim past.

Compared to other German cities, Berlin is quite young and, ironically, began as two cities more than 750 years ago. Museum Island, on the Spree River, was once called Cölln, while the mainland city was always known as Berlin. As early as the 1300s, Berlin prospered from its location at the crossroads of important trade routes. After the ravages of the Thirty Years' War (1618–48), Berlin rose to power as the seat of the Hohenzollern dynasty, as the Great Elector (Friedrich Wilhelm), in his almost 50 years of reign, set off a renaissance in the city, especially in the construction of such academic institutions as the Academy of Arts and the Academy of Sciences. Later, Frederick the Great made Berlin and Potsdam his glorious centers of the enlightened yet autocratic Prussian monarchy.

The German Empire, dominated by Prussia with Berlin as its capital and ruled by the "Iron Chancellor," Count Otto von Bismarck in the late 19th century, proved to be the dominant force in unifying the many independent German principalities. Berlin maintained its status as the imperial German capital throughout the German Empire (1871–1918), the post–World War I Weimar Republic (1919–33), and Hitler's so-called Third Reich (1933–45). But the city's golden years were the Roaring '20s, when Berlin, the energetic, modern, and sinful counterpart to Paris, became a center for the cultural avant-garde. World-famous writers, painters, and artists met here while the impoverished bulk of its 4 million inhabitants lived in heavily overpopulated quarters. This "dance on the volcano," as those years of political and economic upheaval have been called, came to a grisly and bloody end after January 1933, when Adolf Hitler assumed power. The Nazis made Berlin their capital but ultimately failed to remodel the city into a silent monument to their iniquitous power based on fear and terror. During World War II Berlin was bombed to smithereens. At the end of the war, there was more rubble in Berlin than in all other German cities combined.

With the division of Germany after World War II, Berlin was also partitioned—with American, British, and French troops in the districts to the west, and the Soviet Union's forces to the east. With the advent of the cold war in 1947, Berlin became one of the world's hot spots. The three western occupied zones gradually merged, becoming West Berlin, while the Soviet-controlled eastern zone defiantly remained separate. Peace conferences repeatedly failed to resolve the question of Germany's division, and in 1949 the Soviet Union established East Berlin as the capital of its new puppet state, the German Democratic Republic. West Berlin was not legally part of the Federal Republic of Germany, although it was clearly tied to the western Federal Republic's political and economic system. The division of the city was cruelly finalized in concrete in August 1961, when the East German government constructed the infamous Berlin Wall, which broke up families and friendships.

With the wall relegated to the junk pile of history, visitors can appreciate the qualities that mark the city as a whole. Its particular charm has always lain in its spaciousness, its trees and greenery, and its racy atmosphere. When the Greater City of Berlin, as the city-state is known today, was laid out in 1920, entire towns and villages far beyond the downtown area were incorporated. Most of the really stunning parts of the pre-war capital are in the historic eastern part of town, which has grand avenues and monumental buildings, while the western downtown districts possess fancy shopping boulevards.

What really makes Berlin special, however, are the intangibles—the spirit and bounce of the city and its citizens. Berliners come off as brash, witty, no-nonsense types, who speak German with their own piquant dialect and are considered by their fellow countrymen as a most rude species. The bracing air, the renowned *Berliner Luft,* gets part of the credit for their high-voltage energy. It's attributable to the fact that many residents have faced adversity all their lives, and have managed to do so with a mordant wit and cynical acceptance of life.

PLEASURES AND PASTIMES

Beer

The Germans don't just produce *a* beverage called beer; they brew more than 5,000 varieties in a range of tastes and colors. Germany has about 1,300 breweries, 40% of the world's total. The hallmark of the country's dedication to beer is the purity law, *das Reinheitsgebot,* unchanged since Duke Wilhelm IV introduced it in Bavaria in 1516. The law decrees that only malted barley, hops, yeast, and water may be used to make beer, except for specialty wheat beers. Bavaria is the beer-capital of Germany, but Berlin does have its own Berliner Beer. A Berliner Rot (red) or Grün (green) is made by mixing a

Berliner with fruit syrup. For a glossary of German beer, see the Menu Guide.

Construction Sites

It may seem odd, but the latest addition to Berlin's sightseeing highlights is noisy and dirty construction sites. The city's historic downtown area is literally being rebuilt from scratch. Close to US$65 billion will have been spent here by the year 2005. Among the great development projects are the new government district in Tiergarten, between the Reichstag and the Brandenburger Tor, as well as the all-new company headquarters of Sony Europe, debis (Daimler-Benz-Interservices), and Asea Brown Boveri at Potsdamer Platz, some of which are still under construction. The fancy shops at the Friedrichstadtpassagen, including the French department store Galeries Lafayette, on old Friedrichstrasse, are revitalizing one of the city's traditional shopping boulevards, but new arrivals make Friedrichstrasse still worthy of investigating to see buildings in progress.

Lodging

Reassuming its traditional role as a European metropolis, the Berlin of our times continues to attract all major international first-class hotel chains. The latest addition is the Grand Hyatt at Potsdamer Platz. This and other modern luxury resorts are but a faint reminiscence of the pre-war past, when Berlin was considered to be Europe's finest lodging capital. Elegance and style were bombarded to rubbles during World War II, and only a few such havens were rebuilt. Today, for first-class or luxury accommodations, eastern Berlin is easily as good as the western parts of town. If you're seeking something more moderately priced, however, the better choice may be districts like Charlottenburg, Schöneberg, or Wilmersdorf, where there are large numbers of good-value pensions and small hotels; many of them date from the turn of the century, preserving some traditional character.

Museums

Berlin is home to some of the world's most unique museums, art galleries, and exhibition halls. Its more than 100 state and private museums showcase the arts, from ancient times through the medieval and Renaissance periods up to modern avant-garde; historic items of all ages; technology from all over the world; architecture and design of all styles; and nature's treasures. Among the jewels of Berlin's museum culture are original, life-size monuments of Greek, Byzantine, and Roman architecture, on the renowned Museum Island, and the collections of the two Egyptian museums, which include the famous bust of Egyptian queen Nefertiti. In 1999, as museum collections are still being reorganized, some museums and

exhibitions may be closed during certain weeks or months.

Nightlife

Berlin is the only European city without official closing hours, so Berliners and tourists alike enjoy their drinks until the wee hours of the morning without fear of a last call. A peculiar leftover from the bygone days of Allied occupation, liberal handling of drinking hours has transformed Berlin into a nightlife El Dorado. More than 6,000 pubs, music and dancing clubs, cabarets, and theaters guarantee a gamut of fun and entertainment. The city presents Germany's leading dramatic and musical productions, as well as lively variety shows in some of Europe's largest theaters, including the Friedrichstadtpalast. Berlin is also a nightclubbing mecca for acid jazz, drum and bass, and techno music.

HALF-DAY ITINERARIES

In a sprawling city with as many richly stocked museums and curiosities as Berlin, visitors risk seeing half of everything and all of nothing. If you're here for just a short period, these half-day explorations of quintessential Berlin provide a mix of culture, commerce, and relaxation. Whether you're a manic tourist, covering landmarks at a memory-erasing pace, or a hopelessly relaxed traveler, who somehow becomes intimate with the best cafés, but never makes it to the sights you read about while sipping espresso, browse these tours for a guideline. The neighborhood exploring tours in Chapter 2 have more information about the individual sights.

Tour One

This tour's only theme is its variety: palace apartments, sprawling parkland, and pop-up, high-rise construction sites. Start the day sampling the Prussian riches of **Schloss Charlottenburg.** To reach this western palace, take the U-bahn 2 in the direction of Ruhleben to the Bismarckstrasse stop. Transfer to the U-bahn 7 in the direction of Rathaus Spandau. Get off at the next stop, Richard-Wagner-Platz, and walk northwest on Otto-Suher-Allee toward the palace's dome. The total U-bahn ride takes about 15 minutes from Zoologischer Garten. The 18th-century palace's apartments are open for touring, as are the gardens and diverse museums that are either part of the the palace or nearby, like the **Ägyptisches Museum** (Egyptian Museum) and the **Sammlung Berggruen** modern art collection. Limit yourself to 1½ hours here, head back to the U-bahn, and buy some picnic food along the way. When you get to Bismarckstrasse, switch for the U-bahn 2 in the direction of Vinetastrasse and in three stops transfer

once more at Zoologischer Garten for one of the four lines that go to Tiergarten (one stop away). With the efficiency of the German transportation system, this will be a lot smoother than it sounds.

It's time to picnic at **Tiergarten,** the "green lung" of Berlin. In addition to scenic streams, lakes, statues, and landscaped gardens, there's great people-watching here. Turkish families cook up spicy barbecues, friends play soccer, frisbee and badminton, couples sunbathe (nude!); those normally sour-faced Berliners relax on their bicycles or on a walk with their dachshunds. Meander your way eastward, using as landmarks the **Siegessäule** (Victory Column) roundabout and Strasse des 17 Juni, which bisects the park east-west. Exit the park at its southeastern border, and head south.

The cranes you see are racing to meet the millennium at **Potsdamer Platz** (Potsdam Square). Nowhere is any city building so much so fast. Once Berlin's inner-city center, the square withered away within a corner of the Berlin wall. The bright-red Info Box at Leipzigerplatz 21 provides the best overview of the foundation canyons and towering commerical buildings of the future. On weekends the Info box is closed, but you can view the works from Stresemann, Leipziger, and Niederkirchner streets.

Tour Two

Many chic shopping streets are covered here, but consider this either a mellow, introductory browsing tour of the city, or a mid-stay breather. Begin with breakfast or lunch at one of the cafés at Savignyplatz, around which small bookstores and boutiques abound. Stroll south down Bleibtreu or Knesebeck streets and turn left on **Kurfürstendamm,** Berlin's busiest shopping boulevard. As you window shop along tree-lined Ku'damm (Kurfürstendamm's nickname) you'll cross Uhland and Fasanen streets among others before reaching the **Kaiser-Wilhelm-Gedächtniskirche** (Emperor Wilhelm Memorial Church) at Breitscheidplatz.

Along the way, the architecture has been 1950s constructions and restorations of buildings destroyed during World War II. Here, above the plaza's beehive of street musicians, punk kids, and camera-toting tourists, looms a reminder of war's destruction: the hollow, bell tower remains of the church. An adjoining modern church and tower feature concerts and free exhibits, including one on World War II. Next, continue down Ku'damm, which turns into Tauentzien Street. Number 21 is the classy **Kaufhaus des Westens** (KaDeWe), the largest department store in Europe, with a wide selection of foods and snacks on its upper two floors. Grab a treat

here and then board the upper deck of Bus 100, right in front of the store. Check out the new glass dome of the **Reichstag** (Parliament Buildings) as you pass it, and shortly thereafter, get out at the **Brandenburger Tor** (Brandenburg Gate) stop. Once the pride of Berlin, the gate was isolated in the no-man's-land created by the Berlin wall, and then seen in broadcasts around the world when reunited East and West Berliners stood upon the wall behind it. This tour has taken you from west Berlin to east without *too* much walking; from here there are many jumping off points to explore (Tiergarten, Unter den Linden, Friedrichstrasse, Gendarmenmarkt) if you have the time or energy.

Tour Three

Within the narrow confines of the Spree Canal, the **Museumsinsel** (Museum Island) will fill a half day, and even two full days. One of the many humbling treasures of its four world-class museums—the Altes Museum, Alte Nationalgalerie, Pergamonmuseum, and Bodemuseum— is the ancient Greek temple, the Pergamon Altar in the Pergamonmuseum. Deciding how to allocate your time is made somewhat easier by the fact that the Bodemuseum and parts of the Alte Nationalgalerie are closed to the public through 2001. After ogling the museums, follow the canal south to the enormous 19th-century cathedral **Berliner Dom.** The adjacent modern buildings are left over from Communist rule.

Turn left on Karl-Liebknecht-Strasse, as we now return you to the Alexanderplatz S-bahn. On the way, take a look at the 13th-century **St. Marienkirche** and the bordering **Alexanderplatz,** the oversized square that once formed the hub of eastern Berlin's city life. No matter what cranes may pop up during the planned redevelopment of the square, the Fernsehturm, the soaring TV tower, will continue to assert itself 1,198 ft high above the earth. The tower's observation platform offers the best view of Berlin. In case you haven't grabbed a bite to eat at Museumsinsel, you can also take a break at its rotating café.

Visit Museumsinsel Tuesday through Friday (Monday it is closed, and the weekends are extra-crowded). Take the S-bahn to Friedrichstrasse and enter the museum complex at the northwest side of the island, from Am Kupfergraben.

Tour Four

This tour is geographically centered around **Friedrichstrasse,** which has eclipsed the age of Communism to return to its roots as a shopping promenade (it's smaller-scale and calmer than Ku'damm).

Begin at the corner of Unter den Linden and Friedrichstrasse, and head south on Friedrichstrasse. You'll pass craft stores featuring wooden ornaments, figurines and nutcrackers, as well as hotels, bookstores, and designer clothing boutiques. The French department store Galeries Lafayette is at the intersection of Französischestrasse. Its space-age interior steel and glass funnel is worth checking out. Turn left at this corner to reach **Gendarmenmarkt,** one of Europe's finest plazas. Within its pristine borders are the 1818 Schauspielhaus, one of Berlin's main concert hall, and the Deutscher and Französischer Dom (German and French Cathedrals). Pricey sidewalk cafés surround the Gendarmenmarkt. Return to Friedrichstrasse, and walk nine blocks down to **Checkpoint Charlie** at the corner of Friedrichstrasse and Niederkirchenstrasse (you can also take the S-bahn one stop from Französischestrasse to Kochstrasse). This was the most famous crossing point between the two Berlins. Almost nothing here remains from the days of the cold war, but the Haus am Checkpoint Charlie (House at Checkpoint Charlie—The Wall Museum) reviews the thrilling history of the wall, spies, and East German escapes.

2 Exploring Berlin

EXPLORING BERLIN is different from sightseeing in most other German big cities because, as a young and partly planned capital, its streets and boulevards are organized in an unusually clear manner. But Berlin is laid out on an epic scale—western Berlin alone is four times the size of the city of Paris. Although public transportation makes some sightseeing attractions convenient and inexpensive, the sheer magnitude of the city and its wealth of tourist attractions make it hard to reach all of the important sights during a short visit.

There are 23 boroughs in Berlin; for tourists, the three most important are Charlottenburg and Tiergarten in the downtown western area and Mitte in the historic eastern part of town. These take about two days to explore. Three days will allow you a more leisurely pace to appreciate Berlin's dramatic history and exciting present, beyond the traditional tourist highlights. A trip of fewer than five days, however, is not enough time to experience the real, electrifying atmosphere of this city or to visit sights off the beaten track. If you stay here any longer, you may want to remain forever and become a Berliner.

Numbers in the text correspond to numbers in the margin and on the Berlin map.

The Kurfürstendamm and Western Downtown Berlin

The Ku'damm, as Berliners (and most visitors as well) affectionately refer to the Kurfürstendamm, Berlin's busiest shopping street, stretches for 3 km (2 mi) through the heart of the city's western downtown section. The popular thoroughfare is lined with shops, department stores, art galleries, theaters, movie houses, and hotels, as well as some 100 restaurants, bars, clubs, and sidewalk cafés. Berlin's best-known boulevard bustles with shoppers and strollers most of the day and far into the night.

To leisurely shop from the western end of the Kurfürstendamm down to its beginning at Breitscheidplatz takes at least four hours, including a quick breakfast or lunch. You could easily spend at least three hours between observing the culture and counterculture around the Kaiser-Wilhelm-Gedächtniskirche, and combing the shops along the Tauentzien and the KaDeWe. A trip to the zoo and the aquarium will take at least two hours. You won't regret spending less time shopping and more time watching the animals. Be mindful of the strict German store-closing hours and expect the Ku'damm to be extremely crowded on Saturday mornings; everybody is in a rush because most shops close at 2 PM.

Sights to See

❸ Europa Center. This vast shopping and business complex was erected at the site of the renowned Romanisches Café, the hot spot for writers and actors during the Roaring '20s. The 1960s 22-story tower—dubbed "Pepper's Manhattan" after its owner, K. H. Pepper—houses more than 100 shops, restaurants and cafés, two cinemas, a theater, a casino, and the Verkehrsamt (tourist information center). You can even find two pieces of the Berlin Wall by the Tauentzienstrasse entrance. For a spectacular view of the city, take the lift to the i-Punkt restaurant and observation platform on the top floor. Berlin's largest thermal baths are at the top as well. Today, the plaza in front of the Europa Center is a "city within a city," and much more interesting than the somewhat out-of-fashion stores inside. In the summer, Berliners, hippies, homeless people, and tourists mingle on the plaza. ⊠ *Breitscheidpl.*

★ **❷ Kaiser-Wilhelm-Gedächtniskirche** (Emperor Wilhelm Memorial Church). This ruin stands as a dramatic reminder of the war's destruction. The bell tower, which Berliners call "hollow tooth," is all that remains of the once-imposing church, which was built between 1891 and 1895 and originally dedicated to the emperor, Kaiser Wilhelm I. On the hour you'll hear the chimes in the tower play a melody composed by the last emperor's great-grandson, the late Prinz Louis Ferdinand von Hohenzollern.

In stark contrast to the old bell tower are the adjoining Memorial Church and Tower built by famous German architect Professor Egon Eiermann in 1959–61. These ul-

12

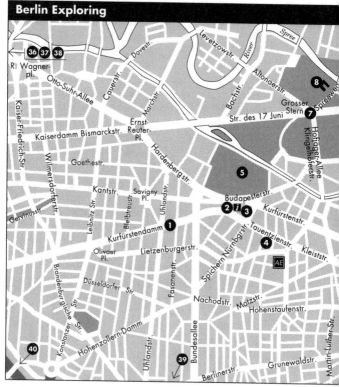

Berlin Exploring

Ägyptisches Museum, **37**

Alexanderplatz, **27**

Berliner Dom, **25**

Berliner Rathaus, **28**

Brandenburger Tor, **10**

Brecht-Weigel-Gedenkstätte, **31**

Checkpoint Charlie, **16**

Dahlem Museums, **39**

Deutsches Historisches Museum, **23**

East Side Gallery, **41**

Europa Center, **3**

Friedrichstrasse, **18**

Gendarmenmarkt, **19**

Grunewald, **40**

Hamburger Bahnhof, **33**

Jüdischer Friedhof, **35**

Kaiser-Wilhelm-Gedächtniskirche, **2**

Kaufhaus des Westens, **4**

Kronprinzenpalais, **22**

Kulturforum, **12**

Kurfürstendamm, **1**

Märkisches Museum, **30**

Museumsinsel, **24**

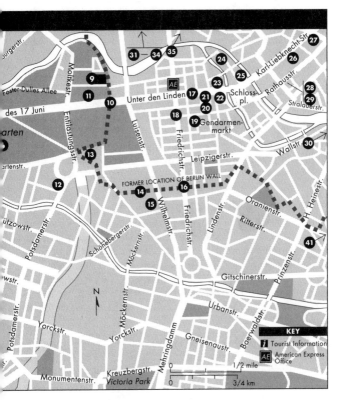

Neue
Synagoge, **32**

Potsdamer
Platz, **13**

Preussischer
Landtag, **14**

Prinz-Albrecht-
Gelände, **15**

Reichstag, **9**

Sachsenhausen
Gedenkstätte, **34**

Sammlung
Berggruen, **38**

St. Hedwigs-
kathedrale, **20**

St.
Marienkirche, **26**

St.
Nikolaikirche, **29**

Schloss
Bellevue, **8**

Schloss
Charlottenburg, **36**

Siegessäule, **7**

Sowjetisches
Ehrenmal, **11**

Staatsoper Unter
den Linden, **21**

Tiergarten, **6**

Unter den
Linden, **17**

Zoologischer
Garten, **5**

tramodern octagonal structures, with their myriad honey-comb windows, are perhaps best described by their nick-names: the lipstick and the powder box. The interior is dominated by the brilliant blue of its stained-glass windows, imported from Chartres, France. Church music and organ concerts are presented in the church regularly.

An historic exhibition inside the old tower focuses on the devastation of World War II, with a religious cross constructed with nails that were recovered from the ashes of the burned-out Coventry Cathedral in England, destroyed in a German bombing raid in November 1940. ⊠ *Breitscheidpl.,* ☎ *030/218–5023.* 🎫 *Free.* ☉ *Old Tower, Mon.–Sat. 10–4; Memorial Church, daily 9–7.*

❹ Kaufhaus des Westens (Department Store of the West). The KaDeWe isn't just Berlin's classiest department store; it's also Europe's biggest department store, a grand-scale emporium in modern guise. An enormous selection of goods can be found on its seven floors, but it is best known for its food and delicatessen counters, restaurants, champagne bars, and beer bars covering the two upper floors, and its crowning rooftop winter garden. ⊠ *Tauentzienstr. 21,* ☎ *030/21–210.*

❶ Kurfürstendamm. This grand boulevard, known locally as Ku'damm, is certainly the liveliest and most exciting stretch of roadway in Berlin. The busy thoroughfare was first laid out during the 16th century as the path by which Elector Joachim II of Brandenburg traveled from his palace on the Spree River to his hunting lodge in the Grunewald. The Kurfürstendamm (Elector's Causeway) was developed into a major route in the late 19th century, thanks to the initiative of Bismarck, the "Iron Chancellor."

Don't look for house Number 1—when the Ku'damm was relocated in the early '20s, the first 10 address numbers were just dropped. Back then, the Ku'damm was a relatively new boulevard and by no means the city's most elegant one; it was fairly far removed from the old heart of the city, which was Unter den Linden in the eastern section of Berlin. The Ku'damm's pre-war fame was due mainly to the rowdy bars and dance halls that studded much of its length and its side streets.

Along with the rest of Berlin, the Ku'damm suffered severe wartime bombing. Almost half of its 245 late-19th-century buildings were destroyed in the 1940s, and the remaining buildings were damaged in varying degrees. What you see today (as in most of western Berlin) is either restored or was constructed during the past decades. Some of the old 1950s buildings are gradually being replaced by modern, futuristic-looking skyscrapers.

★ ♻ ❺ **Zoologischer Garten** (Zoological Gardens). Germany's oldest zoo opened in 1844 and today has become Europe's largest. You'll find it in the southwestern corner of the 630-acre park called the Tiergarten (Animal Garden). After being destroyed during World War II, the zoo was carefully redesigned to create surroundings as close to the animals' natural environment as possible. The zoo houses more than 14,000 animals belonging to 1,700 different species and has been successful in breeding rare species. The picturesque, Asian-style **Elefantentor** (Elephant Gate), which is the main entrance to the zoo at Budapesterstrasse, adjoins the aquarium. ✉ *Hardenbergpl. 8 and Budapester Str. 34,* ☎ *030/254–010.* ▣ *Zoo DM 12, aquarium DM 12, combined ticket to zoo and aquarium DM 19.* ☉ *Zoo Apr.–mid-Oct., daily 9–6:30; late Oct.–Mar., daily 9–5; aquarium daily 9–6.*

NEED A BREAK? Set some time aside for coffee at **Einstein Café** (✉ Kurfürstenstr. 58, ☎ 030/261–5096), where you can select from a variety of exotic coffees. The Viennese-style coffeehouse is in the beautiful 19th-century mansion of German silent-movie star Henny Porten.

The Tiergarten and the Brandenburger Tor

The Tiergarten, a beautifully laid-out park with lakes and paths is the "green lung" of Berlin. In summer it is swamped by sunbathers and families with their barbecues. Its eastern end between the grandiose landmarks of the Reichstag (Parliament) and the Brandenburger Tor (Brandenburg Gate) is currently being developed into the new seat of the federal government.

A Good Walk

From the Zoologischer Garten (☞ *above*), you can set off diagonally through the greenery of idyllic **Tiergarten** ⑥, which served as the hunting grounds of the Great Elector during the 17th century. At the center of the park you'll approach the traffic intersection known as the Grosser Stern (Big Star), so called because five roads meet here. This is the park's highest point and the site of the **Siegessäule** ⑦. Follow the Spreeweg Road from the Grosser Stern to **Schloss Bellevue** ⑧, the seat of the German federal president. Leave the Schloss Bellevue and head east along the John-Foster-Dulles Allee, keeping the Spree River in sight on your left. You'll soon pass the former Kongresshalle (Congress Hall), which houses exhibitions on art and cultures of Third World countries.

Continuing east, you'll reach the monumental **Reichstag** ⑨, the German Empire's old parliament building. Today the historic building is once again housing the German federal parliament, the Deutscher Bundestag. Just south of the Reichstag, where Strasse des 17. Juni meets Unter den Linden, is another monumental symbol of German unity and of the long division of Berlin—the mighty **Brandenburger Tor** ⑩, probably the most significant landmark of both German triumphs and defeats.

A short distance west, along Strasse des 17. Juni—a name that commemorates the 1953 uprising of former East Berlin workers that was quashed by Soviet tanks—you will see the **Sowjetisches Ehrenmal** ⑪. Turn south from the memorial onto the Entlastungsstrasse and cross the tip of the Tiergarten to nearby Kemperplatz, with its **Kulturforum** ⑫, a large square where you'll find a series of fascinating museums and galleries, such as the New National Gallery, and the Philharmonie music hall. At its eastern side behind the **Staatsbibliothek** lies the **Potsdamer Platz** ⑬, still Europe's biggest construction site, where several companies are continuing to erect their headquarters, and others have just opened their business centers and shopping malls. To get a good look at the continuing buildup of concrete and steel, head southeast along Stresemannstrasse. Then follow Niederkirchnerstrasse, tracing the Berlin Wall's former location in this area.

This is yet another strip of German history, with the old **Preussischer Landtag** ⑭, the seat of Berlin's parliament, and the **Prinz-Albrecht-Gelände** ⑮, with the cellar ruins of Nazi SS headquarters. The history of the hideous Berlin Wall can be followed in the museum that arose at the former **Checkpoint Charlie** ⑯ crossing point at Friedrichstrasse, the second cross street heading east on Niederkirchnerstrasse. Almost nothing here remains of the days of the cold war, but the museum tells the fascinating stories of the wall, refugees, and spies.

TIMING

You can do the whole tour in a day, providing you take Berlin's least expensive public-transportation vehicle, Bus 100. It starts at the U-bahn station Zoologischer Garten and has several stops along the Kurfürstendamm and all major streets in the Tiergarten. You can leave and reboard the bus whenever you like. All buildings in the Tiergarten, with the exception of the former Kongresshalle, are closed to the public, so you can explore Tiergarten in less than two hours, even if you walk. The Brandenburger Tor and the Kulturforum won't take long to see either. If you want to spend some time in the museums around Kemperplatz, reserve at least three hours before heading to the Preussischer Landtag and the Prinz-Albrecht-Gelände. Depending on the exhibitions shown, you might stay at those two places for another two hours minimum before exploring the area around Checkpoint Charlie.

Sights to See

Brandenburger Tor (Brandenburg Gate). This massive gate, once the pride of imperial Berlin, was left an eerie no-man's-land when the wall was built. After the wall's demise the gate was the focal point of much celebrating, for this evocative symbol of Berlin was finally returned to all the people of the newly united city. The Brandenburger Tor, the only remaining gate of an original group of 14 built by Carl Langhans in 1788–91, was designed as a triumphal arch for King Frederick Wilhelm II in virile classical style paying tribute to Athens's Acropolis. The quadriga, a chariot drawn by four horses and driven by the Goddess of Peace, was added in 1794. Troops paraded through the gate after successful campaigns—the last time in 1945, when victorious Red Army troops took Berlin. The upper part of the gate, together with its chariot and Goddess of Peace, was destroyed in the war. In 1957 the original molds were discovered in West Berlin, and a new quadriga was cast in copper and presented as a gift to the people of East Berlin—a remarkable and rare instance of cold-war-era East-West cooperation, even though the Prussian Iron Cross on top of it, a symbol of western militarism to East Germans, was only added in 1991. Now, as the century comes to a close, the square behind the gate, the **Pariser Platz,** has regained its traditional, pre-war design. To the left behind the Brandenburg Gate, the United States built its new German embassy in 1996–98 at the very spot where the former American embassy stood prior to 1945. Dresdner Bank has just finished its new company headquarters here as well. The new buildings surrounding the square may seem modern, but the grand design of this historic spot almost looks like 70 years ago. Adding to this impression is Berlin's most famous address, "Unter den Linden No. 1," which has come alive again: the **Hotel Adlon Berlin,** the meeting point of Europe's jet set during the 1920s, has been rebuilt at its old location.

 ⑯ **Checkpoint Charlie.** This was the most famous crossing point between the two Berlins during the cold war; it was here that American and Soviet tanks faced each other during the tense months of the Berlin blockade in 1948–49. The crossing point disappeared along with the wall, but the

★ **Haus am Checkpoint Charlie** (House at Checkpoint Charlie—The Wall Museum) is still there. The museum reviews the history of the events leading up to the construction of the wall and displays actual tools and equipment, records, and photographs documenting methods used by East Germans to cross over to the West. (One of the most ingenious instruments of escape was a miniature submarine.) The new building behind the museum, the **American Business Center,** was erected on the eastern side of the former Iron Curtain. ⊠ *Friedrichstr. 44,* ☎ *030/251–1031.* 🎫 *DM 7.50.* ⊙ *Daily 9 AM–10 PM.*

 NEED A BREAK?   While trying to imagine the former Checkpoint Charlie crossing and the wall, get a window seat at **Café Adler** (⊠

Friedrichstr. 206, ☎ 030/251–8965), which once bumped right up against the wall. The soups and salads are all tasty—and cheap.

 ⑫ Kulturforum (Cultural Forum). With its unique ensemble of museums, galleries, libraries, and the philharmonic hall, the complex is considered one of Germany's cultural jewels. The **Gemäldegalerie,** which opened in 1997, reunites formerly separated collections from east and west Berlin. It is considered to be one of Germany's finest art galleries and houses an extensive selection of European paintings from the 13th to the 18th centuries. Several rooms are reserved for paintings by German masters, among them Dürer, Cranach the Elder, and Holbein. A special collection houses the works of the Italian masters—Botticelli, Titian, Giotto, Lippi, and Raphael—as well as paintings by Dutch and Flemish masters of the 15th and 16th centuries: van Eyck, Bosch, Brueghel the Elder, and van der Weyden. The museum also contains the world's second-largest Rembrandt collection.

A building that opened in 1994 houses the **Kupferstich-kabinett** (Drawings and Prints Collection) and the **Kunst-bibliothek** (Art Library). The exhibitions at the Kupferstichkabinett include European woodcuts, engravings, and illustrated books from the 15th century to the present. Also on display are several pen-and-ink drawings by Dürer, 150 drawings by Rembrandt, and a photographic archive. The Kunstbibliothek contains art posters, a costume library, ornamental engravings, and a commercial art collection. Another building displays paintings dating from the late Middle Ages to 1800. ⊠ *Matthäikirchpl., Gemaldegalerie,* ☎ *030/266–2002; Kupferstichkabinett, 030/266–2030; Kunstbibliothek 030/266–2046.* ▣ *Free; Tageskarte (day card, DM 8) covers 1-day admission to all museums at Kulturforum and is available at all museums.* ⊙ *Tues.–Fri. 9–5, weekends 10–5.*

The roof that resembles a great tent belongs to the **Phil-harmonie** (Philharmonic Hall), home to the renowned Berlin Philharmonic Orchestra since 1963 (☞ Nightlife and the Arts, *below*). The smaller Chamber Music Hall adjoining it was built in 1987. Both these buildings and the

Staatsbibliothek (National Library), one of the largest libraries in Europe, were designed by Hans Scharoun.

The Philharmonie added the **Musikinstrumenten-Museum** (Musical Instruments Museum) in 1984. It is well worth a visit for its fascinating collection of keyboard, string, wind, and percussion instruments. ⊠ *Tiergartenstr. 1, ☎ 030/254–810. ☜ DM 4, free 1st Sun. of every month; tour DM 3. ⊙ Tues.–Fri. 9–5, weekends 10–5; guided tour Sat. at 11; presentation of Wurlitzer organ 1st Sat. of month at noon.*

Inside the **Kunstgewerbemuseum** (Museum of Decorative Arts), which is opposite the Philharmonie, you'll find a display of arts and crafts in Europe from the Middle Ages to the present. Among its notable exhibits are the Welfenschatz (Welfen Treasure), a collection of 16th-century gold and silver plates from Nürnberg, as well as ceramics and porcelains. ⊠ *Matthäikirchpl. 10, ☎ 030/266–2911. ☜ DM 4, free Sun. and holidays. ⊙ Tues.–Fri. 9–5, weekends 10–5.*

The **Neue Nationalgalerie** (New National Gallery) collection comprises paintings, sculptures, and drawings from the 19th and 20th centuries, with an accent on works by such Impressionists as Manet, Monet, Renoir, and Pissarro. Other schools represented are German Romantics, Realists, Expressionists, and Surrealists. In a modern glass-and-steel building designed by Mies van der Rohe and built in the mid-1960s, the gallery frequently showcases outstanding international art exhibitions. ⊠ *Potsdamer Str. 50, ☎ 030/266–2662. ☜ DM 4; free holidays and 1st Sun. of every month. ⊙ Tues.–Fri. 9–5, weekends 10–5.*

❀ ★ ⑬ Potsdamer Platz (Potsdam Square). The once-divided capital is being rejoined on this square, Berlin's former inner-city center, which was Europe's busiest plaza before World War II. Looking at today's constructions of steel, glass, and concrete, it is hard to imagine the square as the no-man's-land it was when the wall cut across it. Where the British, American, and Russian sectors once met, Sony, Mercedes Benz, Asea Brown Boveri, and Hertie are building their new company headquarters. Today, the first buildings are already in use; the two high-rise towers dominating the square are part of the headquarters of debis, the software subsidiary of Mercedes Benz. The **Potsdamer Platz Arkaden,** Berlin's

new and most elegant shopping and entertainment mecca
covering 40,000 square yds, is housing close to 150 upscale
shops, a musical theater, a new variety stage, cafés, a movie
complex with a 3D-IMAX cinema, and even a new casino.
Right next to it is Berlin's newest first-class hotel, the
Grand Hyatt Berlin. The best overview of the ongoing construction is in a futuristic, bright-red Information Center,
which resembles an oversize container, at the eastern end
of the Potsdamer Platz. Its flat roof serves as an open-air
observation deck. English tours of the exhibit are available
by appointment. ☒ *Infobox, Leipziger Pl. 21,* ☎ *030/
2266–2424.* 🎫 *Free, observation deck DM 2.* ☉ *Mon.–
Wed. and Fri. 9–7, Thurs. 9–9, weekends 9–7.*

⑭ Preussischer Landtag (Prussian State Legislature). The monumental parliamentary building on the northern side of
Niederkirchnerstrasse now houses Berlin's House of Deputies
and is one of Germany's most impressive administration
buildings. Even if the House isn't in session, you should take
a look inside and admire the huge entrance hall. Opposite
is the **Martin-Gropius-Bau,** a renowned exhibition hall and
home to a city museum, a gallery of local art, and a museum on Jewish culture in Berlin. Along Niederkirchnerstrasse is one of only four still-standing sections of the
infamous Berlin Wall. ☒ *Niederkirchnerstr. 5,* ☎ *030/
2325–2325.* ☉ *Preussischer Landtag weekdays 8–6 (hours
vary depending on exhibit).*

⑮ Prinz-Albrecht-Gelände (Prince Albrecht Grounds). Buildings here housed the headquarters of the SS, the Main Reich
Security Office, and other Nazi security organizations from
1933 until 1945. After the war the grounds were leveled.
They remained untouched until 1987, when the basements
of the buildings, which were used as so-called house pris-
ons by the SS, were excavated, and an exhibit documenting their history and Nazi atrocities was opened. Tours are
available by appointment. ☒ *Topography of Terror, Stresemannstr. 110,* ☎ *030/254509.* 🎫 *Free.* ☉ *Daily 10–6.*

⑨ Reichstag (Parliament Building). This gray and monolithic-
looking building became world famous when, in the summer of 1995, American artists Christo and Jeanne-Claude
wrapped the traditional seat of German parliament. The

Reichstag was erected between 1884 and 1894 to house the German parliament during the time of the German Empire and later served a similar function during the ill-fated Weimar Republic. On the night of February 28, 1933, the Reichstag and its pompous glass dome were burned to a shell under mysterious circumstances, an event that provided the Nazis with a convenient pretext for outlawing all opposition parties. The Reichstag was rebuilt, but it was again badly damaged in 1945 in the Battle of Berlin, the final struggle between the Red Army and the German Wehrmacht. After extensive remodeling by British architect Sir Norman Foster, who added a new, futuristic glass cupola, the Reichstag is once again hosting the Deutscher Bundestag, Germany's federal parliament. The building is open to the public, and includes an exhibition area and a restaurant and cafeteria under the cupola. At press time, however, opening hours and other visitor information details were still unavailable.

8 **Schloss Bellevue** (Bellevue Palace). This small palace has served as the West German federal president's official residence in West Berlin since 1959. It was built on the Spree River in 1785 for Frederick the Great's youngest brother, Prince August Ferdinand. In 1994 then-president Richard von Weizsäcker made it his main residence. Since then it has been closed to the public. ⊠ *Schloss Bellevue Park.*

7 **Siegessäule** (Victory Column). The 227-ft-high granite, sandstone, and bronze column has a splendid view across much of Berlin. It was originally erected in 1873 to commemorate the successful Prussian military campaigns and was set up in front of the Reichstag. A climb of 285 steps up through the column to the observation platform can be tiring, but the view makes it worth the effort. ⊠ *Am Grossen Stern,* ☎ *030/391–2961.* ✆ *DM 2.* ✆ *Mon. 1– 6, Tues.–Sun. 9–6.*

11 **Sowjetisches Ehrenmal** (Soviet Honor Monument). Built directly after World War II, this semicircular monument stands as a reminder of the bloody Soviet victory over the shattered German army in Berlin in May 1945. The structure, which shows a bronze statue of a soldier, rests on a marble plinth taken from Hitler's former Berlin monumental Reichkanzlei (headquarters). The memorial is flanked by what are said to be the first two T-34 tanks to have fought their way into the city during the last days of the war. ⊠ *Str. des 17. Juni.*

❻ Tiergarten (Animal Garden). For Berliners, the quiet greenery of the Tiergarten is usually the equivalent of what Central Park is to New Yorkers—a green oasis in the heart of urban turmoil. In recent years, however, Berliners often find the tranquility of their beloved park disrupted by bulldozers working their way through the greenery to construct the multibillion-dollar **Nord-Süd-Tunnel** within the park grounds. This tunnel will redirect downtown traffic when the Tiergarten becomes the seat of the new federal government; the tunnel, however, may not be completed for several years. The park with its 6½ acres of lakes and ponds was originally landscaped by famous garden architect Joseph Peter Lenné. During the summer the Tiergarten, with some 23 km (14 mi) of footpaths along white marble sculptures, becomes the epitome of multicultural Berlin: Turkish families frolic in the green meadows and have spicy barbecues, while children play soccer and gay couples sunbathe. In the center of the Tiergarten you'll find the former **Kongresshalle**, nicknamed the "pregnant oyster," because of its balloonlike shape; it's now home to the World Culture House. ⊠ *Kongresshalle: John-Foster-Dulles Allee 10,* ☎ *030/397870.* ☉ *Hours vary depending on exhibitions and festivals.*

Unter den Linden and Historic Berlin

Behind the Brandenburger Tor (Brandenburg Gate; ☞ Tiergarten *and* Brandenburger Tor, *above*), Unter den Linden and Friedrichstrasse, the main streets of eastern Berlin, are full of restored historic landmarks, museums, and new shopping malls. At the very end of this distinguished boulevard, around Alexanderplatz, eastern Berlin's handful of skyscrapers bear witness to a bustling urban atmosphere.

Exploring the historic heart of Berlin might seem just as exhausting as the city's past has been dramatic. The walk down Unter den Linden past Alexanderplatz to the St. Nikolaikirche and the Jewish Quarter takes about two hours if you don't take a close look at any museums or other highlights. You should, however, allow at least the same amount of time for the Museumsinsel. You won't regret one minute of your visit. Most of the other sights, including the museums and cemeteries, can be seen in less than one hour each. If you're short on time, set clear priorities or follow one of the half-day itineraries in Chapter 1. Bear in mind that on weekends, Museumsinsel, Hamburger Bahnhof, and Friedrichstrasse, the Galeries Lafayette in particular, are crowded with tourists, so try to visit there early or during the week.

Sights to See

㉗ Alexanderplatz. This square once formed the hub of East Berlin city life. German writer Alfred Döblin dubbed it the "heart of a world metropolis." It's a bleak sort of place today, open and windswept and surrounded by grimly ugly modern buildings, with no hint of its pre-war bustling activity—a reminder not just of the Allied bombing of Berlin but of the ruthlessness practiced by the East Germans when they demolished the remains of the old buildings. The square, named for Czar Alexander I, and the surrounding area will hardly be recognizable after the completion of a planned radical transformation.

Distinguishing Alexanderplatz from any other part of the city is no problem; just head toward the **Fernsehturm,** the soaring TV tower, completed in 1969 and 1,198 ft high (not accidentally 710 ft higher than western Berlin's broadcasting tower and 98 ft higher than the Eiffel Tower in Paris). The tower's observation platform offers the best view of Berlin; on a clear day you can see for 40 km (25 mi). You can also enjoy a coffee break up there in the city's highest café, which rotates for your panoramic enjoyment. ⊠ *Panoramastr. 1a,* ☎ *030/242–3333.* ☜ *DM 8.* ☾ *Nov.– Apr., daily 10 AM–midnight; May–Oct., daily 9 AM–1 AM.*

★ **㉕ Berliner Dom** (Berlin Cathedral). The impressive 19th-century cathedral, with its enormous green copper dome, is one of the great ecclesiastical buildings in Germany. Its main nave was reopened in June 1993 after a 20-year renovation. There's an observation balcony that allows a view of the cathedral's ceiling and interior. More than 80 sarcophagi of Prussian royals are on display in the cathedral's catacombs. ⊠ *Am Lustgarten,* ☎ *030/202–69136.* ☜

In case you want to see the world.

At American Express, we're here to make your journey a smooth one. So we have over 1,700 travel service locations in over 120 countries ready to help. What else would you expect from the world's largest travel agency?

do more ®

AMERICAN EXPRESS

http://www.americanexpress.com/travel

Travel

In case you want to be welcomed there.

We're here to see that you're always welcomed at establishments everywhere. That's why millions of people carry the American Express® Card – for peace of mind, confidence, and security, around the world or just around the corner.

do more®

Cards

In case you're running low.

We're here to help with more than 118,000 Express Cash locations around the world. In order to enroll, just call American Express before you start your vacation.

do more

And just in case.

We're here with American Express® Travelers Cheques
and Cheques *for Two*.® They're the safest way to carry
money on your vacation and the surest way to get a
refund, practically anywhere, anytime.
Another way we help you...

do more.®

AMERICAN
EXPRESS

Travelers
Cheques

Balcony DM 5, museum free. ☉ *Church Mon.–Sat. 9–6:30, Sun. 11:30–6:30; balcony Mon.–Sat. 10–6, Sun. 11:30–6; museum Wed.–Sun. 10–6.*

Opposite the cathedral on Schlossplatz is a colossal modern building in bronze and mirrored glass—the **Palast der Republik** (Palace of the Republic), a post-war monument to socialist progress that housed East Germany's so-called People's Chamber (parliament). The Palace had been closed since 1991 while politicians tried to find a meaningful use for the asbestos-poisoned building; in the meantime, the building's poisonous materials have been recycled. However, the future use of this unappealing Socialist leftover is still undecided, even though the city launched an international architectural competition for a grand design of both the Schlossplatz and the palace itself. Nothing about the structure and the vast square in front of it suggests that this was the very spot where the Hohenzollern city palace once stood. It was heavily damaged by bombings during the war and was then dynamited by the Communist regime. The smaller building at the southern end of Schlossplatz used to house East Germany's **Staatsrat** (Federal Senate). Ironically, it now serves as the Chancellor's provisional office until the new Chancellery next to the Reichstag is finished sometime in the year 2000. ⊠ *Schlosspl.*

❷❽ **Berliner Rathaus** (Red Town Hall). The former Rotes Rathaus is known for its redbrick design and friezes depicting the city's history. After the city's reunification, this pompous symbol of Berlin's 19th-century urban pride again became the seat of the city government. ⊠ *Jüdenstr. at Rathausstr.,* ☎ *030/24010.* ▣ *Free.* ☉ *Weekdays 7–6.*

❸❶ **Brecht-Weigel-Gedenkstätte** (Brecht-Weigel Memorial Site). You can visit the former working and living quarters of playwright Bertolt Brecht and his wife, Helene Weigel, and there's a library for Brecht scholars. The downstairs restaurant serves Viennese cuisine using Weigel's recipes. Brecht is buried next door, along with his wife and more than 100 other celebrated Germans, in the **Dorotheenstädtischer Friedhof** (Doretheer Cemetery). To get here, take the U-bahn 6 to Oranienburger Tor. Walk north on Friedrichstrasse beyond the bend where the street turns into the Chausseestrasse. ⊠ *Chaussestr. 125,* ☎ *030/282–9916, 030/461–7279* *cemetery.* ✉ *Apartment DM 4, library free.* ☉ *Apartment Tues.–Fri. 10–noon, Thurs. 10–noon and 5–7, Sat. 9:30–noon and 12:30–2, tours every ½ hr; library Tues.–Fri. 9–3; cemetery daily 8–4.*

㉓ Deutsches Historisches Museum (German History Museum). The onetime Prussian arsenal (Zeughaus), a magnificent Baroque building constructed 1695–1730, houses Germany's National History Museum. The oldest building on Unter den Linden, it was used as a hall of fame glorifying Prusso-German militarism. The museum's permanent exhibit provides a compendium of German history from the Middle Ages to the present. Tours are available by appointment. ✉ *Unter den Linden 2,* ☎ *030/215–020.* ✉ *Free, English-speaking guide DM 60.* ☉ *Thurs.–Tues. 10–6.*

★ **⑱ Friedrichstrasse.** There's probably no other street in the whole of eastern Germany that has changed as dramatically as Friedrichstrasse. The once-bustling Fifth Avenue of Berlin's pre-war days has risen from the rubble of war and Communist negligence to recover its glamour of old, though it doesn't offer the sheer number of establishments at the competing Ku'damm.

Heading south on Friedrichstrasse, you'll pass various new business buildings, including the **Lindencorso** and the **Rosmarin-Karree,** which are worth a look both for their architecture and fancy shops. The jewel of this street, however, is the **Friedrichstadtpassagen,** a gigantic shopping and business complex of three buildings praised for their completely different designs. All the buildings are connected by an underground mall of elegant shops and eateries. At the corner of Französische Strasse one of Berlin's most daring new buildings, designed by French star architect Jean Nouvel, houses the French department store **Galeries Lafayette.** Its interior is dominated by a huge steel and glass funnel surrounded by six floors of upscale shopping. The Lafayette, though six times smaller than Berlin's traditional KaDeWe, has become the city's favorite (and most elegant) shopper's paradise. ✉ *Französische Str. 23,* ☎ *030/209–480.*

NEED A BREAK? With Berlin's increasing cosmopolitanism, the symbols of the world's jet set are finding their way into the city. **Planet Hollywood** (✉ Friedrichstrasse 68, ☎ 030/2094–5820), a restaurant chain operated by action stars Bruce Willis, Arnold Schwarzenegger, and Sylvester Stallone, offers light Californian cuisine and good old Austrian apple pie, allegedly prepared from a recipe by Arnie's mother. Among the memorabilia on display is Schwarzenegger's leather outfit from the movie *Terminator 2* and Liz Taylor's headdress from *Cleopatra*.

★ ⓳ **Gendarmenmarkt.** One of Europe's finest piazzas, this large square is the site of the beautifully reconstructed 1818 **Schauspielhaus,** one of Berlin's main concert halls, and the **Deutscher and Französischer Dom** (German and French Cathedrals). The French cathedral contains the **Hugenottenmuseum,** with exhibits charting the history and art of the Protestant refugees from France—the Huguenots—expelled at the end of the 17th century by King Louis XIV. Their energy and commercial expertise did much to help boost Berlin during the 18th century. ⊠ *Gendarmenmarkt,* ☎ *030/229–1760.* ⊡ *DM 3.* ⊙ *Tues.–Sat. noon–5, Sun. 11–5.*

Completed in 1996, the restored **Deutscher Dom** has an extensive historical exhibition sponsored by the Bundestag, the German parliament. It's worth a visit if you're interested in an official view of German history with a particular accent on the Cold War and the division of Germany. If you don't read any German, the exhibits will be a bit hard to follow. ⊠ *Gendarmenmarkt 1,* ☎ *030/2273–2141.* ⊡ *Free.* ⊙ *Tues.–Sun. 10–5.*

★ ㉝ **Hamburger Bahnhof, Museum für Gegenwart–Berlin** (Museum of Contemporary Art). This museum, which opened in 1996, is perhaps the best place to visit in Berlin for a survey of Western art after 1960. The early 19th-century Hamburger Bahnhof building originally served as a train station. When it was remodeled, it received a huge and spectacular new wing, designed by Berlin architect J. P. Kleihues. That addition is alone worth a visit for its stunning interplay of glass, steel, colorful decor, and sunlight coming through skylights. The museum houses the outstanding collection of Berlin businessman Dr. Erich Marx, as well as many items from Berlin's state museums. You can see installations by German artists Joseph Beuys and Anselm Kiefer as well as paintings by Andy Warhol, Cy Twombly,

Robert Rauschenberg, and Robert Morris. ✉ *Invalidenstr. 50–51*, ☎ *030/397–8340.* ✆ *DM 12.* ☉ *Tues.–Fri. 10–6, weekends 11–6.*

㉟ Jüdischer Friedhof (Jewish Cemetery). More than 150,000 graves make this peaceful retreat in Berlin's Weissensee District Europe's largest Jewish cemetery. The cemetery and tombstones are in excellent condition—a seeming impossibility, given its location in the heart of the Third Reich. To reach the Weissensee cemetery, take Tram 2, 3, 4, or 13 from Hackescher Markt to Berliner Allee and head south on Herbert-Baum-Strasse. ☎ *030/965–3330.* ☉ *Sun.–Thurs. 8–4, Fri. 8–3.*

㉒ Kronprinzenpalais (Prince's Palace). Now used as a government guest house, this magnificent building designed in the baroque style was originally constructed in 1732 by Philippe Gerlach for Crown Prince Friedrich (who later became Frederick the Great) and was chosen as the new federal president's seat in the German capital. But after a long legal dispute with the owner of the adjacent Opernpalais, the government gave up its plans and made Schloss Bellevue its first choice. ✉ *Unter den Linden 3.*

㉚ Märkisches Museum (Museum of Brandenburg). At this showcase for Berlin's history, you can see exhibits on the city's theatrical past and a fascinating collection of mechanical musical instruments. They are demonstrated on Sunday at 11 and Wednesday at 3. ✉ *Am Köllnischen Park 5*, ☎ *030/308–660.* ✆ *DM 3, instrument demonstration DM 2.* ☉ *Tues.–Sun. 10–6.*

★ **㉔ Museumsinsel** (Museum Island). On the site of one of Berlin's two original settlements, Cölln, this unique complex of four world-class museums is an absolute must—and not just for museum buffs. The **Altes Museum** (Old Museum) is an austere neoclassical building just north of old Lustgarten that features post-war East German art; its large etching and drawing collection, from the Old Masters to the present, is a treasure trove. The **Alte Nationalgalerie** (Old National Gallery, entrance on Bodestrasse) houses an outstanding collection of 18th-, 19th-, and early 20th-century paintings and sculptures and often hosts special temporary exhibits. Works by Cézanne, Rodin, Degas, and one of Germany's most famous portrait artists, Max Liebermann, are part of the permanent exhibition.

★ Even if you aren't generally interested in exhibits about the ancient world, make an exception for the **Pergamonmuseum** (entrance on Am Kupfergraben). It is not only the stand-out in this complex, but one of the world's greatest muse-ums. The museum's name is derived from its principal and best-loved display, the Pergamon Altar, a monumental Greek temple discovered in what is now Turkey and dat-ing from 180 BC. Equally impressive is the Babylonian Pro-cessional Way in the Asia Minor department.

Last in the complex, with an entrance on Monbijoubrücke, is the **Bodemuseum,** with its superb Egyptian, Byzantine, and early Christian relics, sculpture collections, and coin gallery. The Sphinx of Hatshepsut, from around 1500 BC, is stunning, as are the Burial Cult Room and the world's largest papyrus collection.

Entrance at ⊠ Am Kupfergraben. Museumsinsel: ☎ 030/ 209–050. ▣ Each museum on Museum Island DM 4, Pergamon Museum DM 8, 1st Sun. of every month; Tageskarte (day card, DM 8), available at each museum, covers 1-day admission to all museums. ☉ All museums Tues.–Sun. 10–6.

Please note: Due to reconstructions and a major reorgani-zation of the Museum Island's collections, the Bodemuseum and parts of the Alte Nationalgalerie will be closed to the public through the year 2001.

★ ㉜ **Neue Synagoge** (New Synagogue). This meticulously re-stored landmark, built between 1859 and 1866, is an ex-otic amalgam of styles, the whole faintly Middle Eastern. When its doors opened it was the largest synagogue in Eu-rope, with 3,200 seats. The synagogue was largely ruined on the night of November 9, 1938, the infamous Kristall-nacht (Night of the Broken Glass), when Nazi looters ram-paged across Germany, burning synagogues and smashing the few Jewish shops and homes left in the country. Fur-ther destroyed by Allied bombing in 1943, it remained un-touched until restoration began under the East German regime in the mid-'80s. Its interior was partially restored and reopened in 1995, while its facade was restored between 1983–1990. The building is connected to the modern **Centrum Judaicum,** a center for Jewish culture and learning that frequently stages exhibitions and other cultural events. ✉ *Oranienburger Str. 28/30,* ☎ *030/2840–1316.* ☺ *Sun.–Thurs. 10–6, Fri. 10–2.*

The area to the northeast of the synagogue is known as the **Scheunenviertel** (Stable Quarters), or Jüdisches Viertel (Jewish Quarter). During the second half of the 17th century, the Great Elector brought artisans, small-businessmen, and Jews into the country to improve his financial situation. As industrialization intensified, the quarter became poorer, and in the 1880s many East European Jews escaping pogroms settled here. By the 20th century the quarter had a number of bars, stores, and small businesses frequented by gamblers, prostitutes (they're still here, along Oranienburger Strasse), and poor customers from the area. Since 1989, Jewish religious and business life, which both flourished here until 1933, have gradually reestablished themselves in the historic quarter.

NEED A BREAK?   For coffee, cake, or an Israeli snack of eggplant and pita bread, stop at the **Beth Café** (✉ Tucholskystr. 40, ☎ 030/ 281-3135), one of the first Jewish businesses to open in the city's former Jewish district. The place is small and always full, so be prepared to share a table. Just around the corner from the synagogue, the café is run by the Adass Jisroel Jewish community.

❷⓿ **St. Hedwigskathedrale** (St. Hedwig's Cathedral). Similar to the Pantheon in Rome, this substantial, circular building is Berlin's premier Catholic church. When the cathedral was erected in 1747, it was the first Catholic church built in resolutely Protestant Berlin since the Reformation during the 16th century. Frederick the Great thus tried to silence Prussia's Catholic population after his invasion of Catholic Silesia. ✉ *Hinter der Katholischen Kirche 3,* ☎ *030/203–4810.* ☺ *Weekdays 10–5, Sun. 1–5.*

❷❻ **St. Marienkirche** (St. Mary's Church). This medieval church, one of the finest in Berlin, is worth a visit for its late-Gothic fresco *Der Totentanz* (*Dance of Death*). Obscured for many years, it was restored in 1950, revealing the original in all its macabre allure. The cross on top of the church tower was an everlasting annoyance to Communist rulers, as its golden metal was always mirrored in the windows of the Fernsehturm TV tower, the pride of socialist construction genius. ⊠ *Karl-Liebknecht-Str. 8.,* ☎ *030/242–4467.* ⌑ *Tour free.* ☉ *Mon.–Thurs. 10–noon and 1–5, Sat. noon– 4:30, Sun. noon–5; tour Mon.–Thurs. at 1, Sun. at 11:45.*

㉙ St. Nikolaikirche (St. Nicholas Church). The complex of buildings centering around this medieval twin-spire church gives you an idea of what the old Berlin looked like. The quarter with its tiny cobblestone streets that has grown around Berlin's oldest parish church, dating from 1230, is filled with stores, cafés, and restaurants. The adjacent **Fischerinsel** (Fisherman's Island) area was the heart of Berlin 750 years ago, and today retains some of its medieval character. At Breite Strasse you'll find two of Berlin's oldest buildings: No. 35 is the Ribbeckhaus, the city's only surviving Renaissance structure, dating from 1624, and No. 36 is the early baroque Marstall, built by Michael Matthais from 1666 to 1669. ⊠ *Nikolaikirchpl.,* ☎ *030/2380–900.* ⌑ *DM 3.* ☉ *Tues.–Sun. 10–6.*

㉑ Staatsoper Unter den Linden (State Opera). The lavishly restored opera house, Berlin's prime opera stage, lies at the heart of the Forum Fridericianum. This ensemble of surrounding buildings was designed by Frederick the Great himself to showcase the splendor of his enlightened rule. A performance at the opera house with its maestro, Daniel Barenboim, is often memorable. ⊠ *Unter den Linden 7,* ☎ *030/2035–4555.* ☉ *Box office weekdays 10–6, weekends 2–6; reservations by phone weekdays 10–8, weekends 2–8.*

NEED A BREAK? The **Opernpalais** (⊠ Unter den Linden 5, ☎ 030/202–683) right next to the opera house is home to four different restaurants and cafés, all famous for their rich German cakes, pastries, and brunches.

⑰ Unter den Linden. Thanks to several new buildings, the central thoroughfare of old Berlin has slowly transformed back into the elegant avenue it was during pre-war times.

Its name means "under the linden trees"—no wonder Marlene Dietrich once sang: "As long as the old linden trees still bloom, Berlin is still Berlin." Among the sightseeing attractions worth visiting on Unter den Linden are the ☞ **Kronprinzenpalais,** the ☞ **Deutsches Historiches Museum,** and **Humboldt-Universität** (Humboldt University), originally built in 1766 as a palace for the brother of Friedrich II of Prussia. It became a university in 1810, and Karl Marx and Friedrich Engels were once among its students. The main hall of the university (⌧ Unter den Linden 6, ☎ 030/20930) is open Monday–Saturday 6 AM–10 PM.

Adjacent to the University is the **Neue Wache** (New Guardhouse). Constructed in 1818, it served as the Royal Prussian War Memorial until the declaration of the Weimar Republic in 1918. Badly damaged in World War II, it was restored by the East German state and rededicated in 1960. After unification it was restored to its Weimar Republic appearance and, in November 1993, inaugurated as Germany's central war memorial.

Palaces and Parks in Outer Berlin

Berlin might appear to be a highly energetic city, but beyond its inner district, it is surprisingly green and idyllic. In addition to the Tiergarten, there are several palaces, parks, and museums in the southwestern parts of town that are well worth a visit.

A Good Tour

Besides Berlin's main attractions in the western downtown and eastern historic district, the city has sightseeing spots in outlying areas to the south, the east, and the north that should not be missed. In the far west of the Charlottenburg District lies the baroque palace that gave this part of town its name: **Schloss Charlottenburg** ㊱, with its museums, and the adjacent **Ägyptisches Museum** ㊲ and the **Sammlung Berggruen** ㊳. To get to Schloss Charlottenburg from western downtown Berlin, take the U-bahn 2 from Wittenbergplatz or Zoologisher Garten station in the direction of Ruhleben. Get off at the Bismarckstrasse stop and then take the U-bahn 7 in the direction of Rathaus Spandau to Richard-Wagner-Platz station. From here, walk northwest on Otto-Suher-Allee toward the dome of the palace. The total U-bahn ride takes about 15 minutes.

South of Berlin is a cluster of fine museums, known as the **Dahlem Museums** ㊴, which include the outstanding Museum für Völkerkunde (Ethnographic Museum). The best way to get there from downtown Berlin is by the U-bahn 1 to Dahlem Dorf station. To reach the Dahlem Museums from Schloss Charlottenburg, walk to Richard-Wagner-Platz station and ride the U-bahn 7 in the direction of Rudow until you reach the stop Fehrbelliner Platz. Change trains here and take U-bahn 1 in the direction of Krumme Lanke, getting off at Dahlem Dorf. The trip from the palace to the museums takes about a half hour.

From the Dahlem Museums, it is a short ride via the U-bahn 1 line to the Krumme Lanke station. Change trains at the suburban railway station at nearby Mexikoplatz and take a ride on the S-bahn 3 (in the direction of Potsdam Stadt) or 7 (in the direction of Wannsee) to the Nikolassee, Wannsee, or Grunewald stations. Each serves as a starting point for hour-long hikes through the greenbelt of the **Grunewald** ㊵ and the Wannsee lakes.

It's quite a ride on the S-bahn line toward the east and the **East Side Gallery** ㊶, with a remaining section of the Berlin Wall; there are more than a hundred paintings on the once-infamous concrete. From Wannsee, take S-bahn 3 (in the direction of Erkner) or 7 (in the direction of Ahrensfelde). Leave the train at Hauptbahnhof and walk toward the Spree, to the southern end of Strasse der Pariser Commune, to reach the East Side Gallery. The trip from Wannsee to the gallery will take between 45 minutes and an hour.

Finally, you can make a trip to Sachsenhausen, 35 km (22 mi) north of Berlin, where you'll find the **Sachsenhausen Memorial** ㉞, the only Nazi concentration camp near Berlin. To reach Sachsenhausen, take the suburban S-bahn 1 from Friedrichstrasse to Oranienburg, the last stop. The ride will take 45 to 50 minutes. From the station it's a 25-minute walk, or you can take a taxi. To reach Sachsenhausen from the East Side Gallery, take any S-bahn (3, 5, 7, or 9) from Hauptbahnhof to Friedrichstrasse, and then change

trains to Line 1, getting off at Oranienburg. The trip from
Hauptbahnhof to Oranienburg lasts about an hour.

TIMING

To take in all the attractions above, you will need at least
two full days, with one of them devoted to Schloss Charlottenburg, the Dahlem Museums, and the Grunewald area
alone. A second day may be spent seeing the sights in the
east and north of Berlin. If you skip the museums at Schloss
Charlottenburg and Dahlem, you will still need a full day
to visit the other places.

Sights to See

㊲ Ägyptisches Museum (Egyptian Museum). The former
east guardhouse and residence of the king's bodyguard is
now home to the famous portrait bust of the exquisite
Queen Nefertiti. The 3,300-year-old sculpture of the
Egyptian queen is the centerpiece of a collection of works
that spans Egypt's history since 4000 BC and includes
some of the best-preserved mummies outside Cairo. The
museum is across from ☞ **Schloss Charlottenburg.** ✉
Schlossstr. 70, ☎ *030/320–911.* 🎫 *DM 8.* ☉ *Mon.–
Thurs. 9–6, weekends 10–6.*

㊴ Dahlem Museums. This unique complex of six museums includes the Museum fur Völkerkunde (Ethnographic Museum) and the Skulpturensammlung (Sculpture Collection).
The **Museum für Völkerkunde** is internationally famous for
its arts and artifacts from Africa, Asia, the South Seas, and
the Americas. The large collection of Mayan, Aztec, and
Incan ceramics and stone sculptures should not be missed.
The **Skulpturensammlung** houses Byzantine and European
sculpture from the 3rd through the 18th century. Included
in its collection is Donatello's *Madonna and Child,* sculpted
in 1422. *Museum für Völkerkunde,* ✉ *Lansstr. 8; Skulpturensammlung,* ✉ *Arnimallee 23–27;* ☎ *030/83011.* 🎫
*Museum für Völkerkunde DM 4, Skulpturensammlung
DM 4, free Sun. and holidays.* ☉ *Tues.–Fri. 9–5, weekends 10–5.*

Please note: Due to the reorganization of Berlin's major state
museums, both the Museum für Völkerkunde and the
Skulpturensammlung, as well as parts of the other four museums at the Dahlem location, will be closed in 1999.

❹ East Side Gallery. This section of concrete amounts to nothing less than the largest open-air gallery in the world. Between February and June of 1990, 118 artists from around the globe created unique works of art on the longest—1.3 km (.8 mi)—remaining section of the Berlin Wall; it has been declared an historic monument. One of the most well-known works, by Russian artist Dmitri Vrubel, depicts Brezhnev and Honnecker (the former East German leader) kissing, with the caption "My God. Help me survive this deadly love." ✉ *Mühlenstr./Oberbaumbrücke.* ☉ *Summer, daily 10–5; fall–spring, weekends 10–5.*

❹ Grunewald (Green Forest). Together with its Wannsee lakes, this splendid forest is the most popular green retreat for Berliners. On weekends in spring and fall and daily in summer, Berliners come out in force, swimming, sailing their boats, tramping through the woods, and riding horseback. In winter a downhill ski run and even a ski jump operate on the modest slopes of Teufelsberg Hill. In no other European city has such an expanse of uninterrupted natural surroundings been preserved. Excursion steamers ply the water wonderland of the Wannsee, the Havel River, and the Müggelsee. (☞ Guided Tours *in* Essential Information.)

❸ Sachsenhausen Gedenkstätte (Sachsenhausen Memorial). The only Nazi concentration camp near the Third Reich capital was established in 1936, later becoming a Soviet internment and prison camp for German soldiers. In 1961 the camp was made into a memorial to its more than 100,000 victims. The area has a few preserved facilities and barracks, as well as a memorial and museum. ✉ *Oranienburg, Str. der Nationen 22,* ☎ *03301/803–719.* ▣ *Free.* ☉ *Summer, Tues.–Sun. 8:30–6; winter, Tues.–Sun. 8:30–4:30.*

★ ❸ Sammlung Berggruen (Berggruen Collection). This small museum, which opened in 1996 in the historic Stüler-Bau, focuses on the history of modern art, with representative work from such artists as Van Gogh and Cézanne, Picasso, Giacometti, Klee, and more contemporary artists. Heinz Berggruen, a businessman who emigrated to the United States in the 1930s, collected the excellent paintings on display. This intimate museum has become one of Berlin's most beloved art venues. ✉ *Schlossstr. 1,* ☎ *030/3269–580.* ▣ *DM 8.* ☉ *Tues.–Fri. 9–5, weekends 10–5.*

●36 **Schloss Charlottenburg** (Charlottenburg Palace). This show-
place of western Berlin, the most monumental reminder of
imperial days, served as a city residence for the Prussian
rulers. You can easily spend a full day at Charlottenburg.
In addition to the apartments of the Prussian nobility, you
may explore the landscaped gardens and several excellent
museums set within and just outside the grounds.

The gorgeous palace started as a modest royal summer residence in 1695, built on the orders of King Friedrich I for
his wife, Queen Sophie-Charlotte. During the 18th century,
Frederick the Great made a number of additions, such as
the dome and several wings designed in the rococo style.
By 1790 the complex had evolved into the massive royal
domain you see today. The palace was severely damaged
during World War II but has been painstakingly restored.
Many of the original furnishings and works of art sur-
vived the war and are now on display. Behind heavy iron
gates the Court of Honor—the courtyard in front of the
palace—is dominated by a fine baroque statue, the Reit-
erstandbild des Grossen Kurfürsten (the equestrian statue
of the Great Elector).

Inside the main building the suites of Friedrich I and his
wife are furnished in the prevailing style of the era. Paintings include royal portraits by Antoine Pesne, a noted court
painter of the 18th century. On the first floor you can visit
the Oak Gallery, the early 18th-century palace chapel, and
the suites of Friedrich Wilhelm II and Friedrich Wilhelm
III, furnished in the Biedermeier style.

A gracious staircase leads up to the sumptuous state dining
room and the 138-ft-long **Goldene Galerie** (Golden Gallery).
West of the staircase are the rooms of Frederick the Great,
in which the king's extravagant collection of works by Wat-
teau, Chardin, and Pesne are displayed. Also in the so-called
New Wing is the **Galerie der Romantik** (Gallery of Roman-
ticism), the National Gallery's collection of masterpieces
from such 19th-century German painters as Karl Friedrich
Schinkel and Caspar David Friedrich, the leading member
of the German Romantic school. Visits to the royal apartments are by guided tour only; tours leave every hour on the
hour from 9 to 4. Parks and gardens can be visited for free

and offer a pleasant respite from sightseeing. ✉ *Luisenpl.,* ☎ *030/320–911.* 🖼 *Galerie der Romantik DM 8, guided tour DM 15.* 🕑 *Tues.–Fri. 9–5, weekends 10–5.*

The **Antikensammlung** (antique collection), in the former west guardhouse, is home to a collection of ceramics and bronzes as well as everyday utensils from ancient Greece and Rome and a number of Greek vases from the 6th to the 4th century BC.

The **Museum für Vor- und Frügeschichte** (Museum of Pre- and Early History) depicts the stages of the evolution of humanity from 1 million BC to the Bronze Age. It is in the western extension of the palace opposite Klausener Platz. ☎ *030/ 320–911.* 🖼 *Antikensammlung DM 8, Museum für Vor- und Frügeschichte DM 8; free first Sun.; Tageskarte (day card, DM 15), available at each museum, covers 1-day admission to all museums plus guided tour of Schloss Charlottenburg.* 🕑 *Mon.–Thurs. and weekends 10–6.*

The **park** behind the palace was laid out beginning in 1697 as a baroque French (its only remains are near the palace) and was transformed into an English garden in the early 19th century. There are several buildings in the park that deserve particular attention, including the Belvedere, a teahouse (overlooking the lake and Spree River) that now houses a collection of Berlin porcelain, and the Schinkel Pavilion behind the palace near the river.

3 Dining

AS IN FEW OTHER GERMAN CITIES, dining in Berlin can either mean sophisticated nouvelle specialties in upscale restaurants with linen tablecloths and hand-painted porcelain plates or hearty local specialties in atmospheric and inexpensive inns; the range is as vast as the city itself. Specialties include *Eisbein mit Sauerkraut* (knuckle of pork with pickled cabbage), *Rouladen* (rolled stuffed beef), *Spanferkel* (suckling pig), *Berliner Schüsselsülze* (potted meat in aspic), *Schlachterplatte* (mixed grill), *Hackepeter* (ground beef), and *Kartoffelpuffer* (fried potato cakes). Spicy *Currywurst* is a chubby frankfurter that's served in a variety of ways at *Bockwurst* stands all over the city. Turkish specialties are an integral part of the Berlin food scene. On almost every street you'll find snack stands selling *Döner Kepab* (grilled lamb with salad in a flat-bread pocket).

Eating on the Go

Butcher shops, known as *Metzgerei*, often have a corner that serves warm snacks like *Bouletten* or *Currywurst*.

We recommend cafeterialike restaurants in **department stores** for their wholesome, appetizing, and inexpensive food. Kaufhof, Karstadt, Horton, and Hertie are names to note, as well as the enormous KaDeWe.

Imbiss, or **stand-up snack bars,** are located in pedestrian zones, and found in almost every busy shopping street, in parking lots, train stations, and near markets. They serve *Würste* (sausages), grilled, roasted, or boiled, of every shape and size, and rolls filled with cheese, cold meat, or fish. Prices range from DM 3 to DM 6 per portion.

Restaurants

CATEGORY	COST*
$$$$	over DM 100
$$$	DM 75–DM 100
$$	DM 50–DM 75
$	under DM 50

*per person for a three-course meal, excluding drinks

$$$$ ✕ **Bamberger Reiter.** One of the city's leading restaurants,
★ Bamberger is presided over by Tyrolean chef Franz Rane-
burger. He relies on fresh market produce for his *Neue
Deutsche Küche* (new German cuisine), so the menu changes
daily. ⊠ *Regensburgerstr. 7,* ☎ *030/218–4282. Reservations essential. AE, DC, V. Closed Sun., Mon., and Jan. 1–
15. No lunch.*

$$$$ ✕ **Rockendorf's.** The city's premier restaurant only has
★ fixed-price menus, some with up to nine courses. Exquisitely
presented on fine porcelain, the mainly nouvelle specialties
are sometimes fused with classic German cuisine. The wine
list—with 800 choices, one of the world's best—has the appropriate accompaniment to any menu. ⊠ *Düsterhaupt-
str. 1,* ☎ *030/402–3099. Reservations essential. AE, DC,
MC, V. Closed Sun., Mon., Dec. 25–Jan. 6, and 3–4 wks
in summer.*

$$$ ✕ **Alt-Luxemburg.** In the Charlottenburg District, this pop-
★ ular restaurant is tastefully furnished, and attentive service
enhances the intimate setting. Chef Karl Wannemacher
uses only the freshest ingredients for his French-German
dishes, including his divine lobster lasagna. ⊠ *Windscheid-
str. 31,* ☎ *030/323–8730. AE, DC, V. Closed Sun.*

$$$ ✕ **Borchardt.** This is one of the most fashionable of the meet-
★ ing places that have sprung up in historic Berlin. The high
ceiling, columns, red plush benches, and art nouveau mosaic (discovered during renovations) help create the impression of a 1920s café where today's celebrities meet. The
cuisine is high-quality French-Mediterranean, including a
lot of dishes with fresh fish and veal, such as *Kalbsrück-
ensteak mit Zitronenbutter und grünen Bohnen* (veal steak
with lemon butter and green beans). ⊠ *Französische Str.
47,* ☎ *030/203–97117. Reservations essential. AE, V.*

$$$ ✕ **Paris Bar.** Just off the Ku'damm, this trendy restaurant
attracts a polyglot clientele of film stars, artists, en-
trepreneurs, and executives who care more for glamour than
gourmet food. The cuisine, including such delights as
Jacques oysters and lamb chops with Provençal herbs, is
high-powered, medium-quality French. ⊠ *Kantstr. 152,*
☎ *030/313–8052. AE.*

$$$ ✕ **Tucci.** This Italian restaurant, where light dishes and high-
★ quality Italian brunches are served along with fine wines,
is still a well-kept secret. The service is friendly and quick;

in summer you can sit down at one of their outside tables and enjoy people-watching. Ask for their specials of the day. ✉ *Grolmanstr. 52*, ☎ *030/313–9335. No credit cards.*

$$$ ✕ **VAU.** Still a newcomer to Berlin's hip restaurant scene, ★ the VAU surprised everybody with its excellent German fish and game dishes prepared by chef Kolja Kleeberg, who was just granted a Michelin star. Among his creations are daring combinations such as *Lammhaxe mit Schmorgemüse* (leg of lamb with braised vegetables) and *Steinbutt mit Kalbbries auf Rotweinschalotten* (turbot with veal sweetbread on shallots in red wine). The VAU's cool interior is all style and modern art—small wonder, though: it was designed by one of Germany's leading industrial designers, Peter Schmidt. ✉ *Jägerstr. 54/55*, ☎ *030/2029–730. Reservations essential. AE, DC, MC, V. Closed Sun.*

$$ ✕ **Französischer Hof.** The ceilings in this classy restaurant are high, and the wine list is long. International fare, with an emphasis on French dishes, is served with impeccable service. The maître d' claims guests can find "an oasis of calm and relaxation" here, and he's right. The summer terrace offers a seat practically on the Gendarmenmarkt. ✉ *Jägerstr. 56*, ☎ *030/204–3570. AE, DC, MC, V.*

$$ ✕ **Grossbeerenkeller.** The cellar restaurant, with its mas-★ sive, dark-oak furniture and decorative antlers, has been known for its popularity among Berlin politicians. It's undoubtedly one of the most original dining spots in town, exuding an old-fashioned, warm Berlin hospitality hard to find elsewhere these days. Owner and bartender Ingeborg Zinn-Baier presents such dishes as *Sülze vom Schweinekopf mit Bratkartoffeln und Remoulade* (diced pork with home fries and herb sauce), *Kasseler Nacken mit Grünkohl* (boiled salt pork meat with green cabbage), and other traditional Berlin dishes. Her fried potatoes, by the way, are said to be the best in town. Don't ask for recipes, though: for two generations, they have been a well-kept secret of her family. ✉ *Grossbeerenstr. 90*, ☎ *030/2513–064. No credit cards. Closed Sun. and holidays.*

$$ ✕ **März.** Come here for nouvelle German and Continental cuisine at its best. The creative concoctions include fresh homemade pasta with organic spinach leaves. It's near the New National Gallery, overlooking the Schöneberger Ufer. Because this is a relatively small place, ask for a table in the

## 42

Berlin Dining

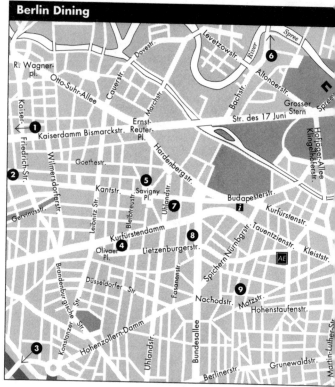

Alt-Luxemburg, **2**
Alt-Cöllner Schankstuben, **18**
Bamberger Reiter, **9**
Blockhaus Nikolskoe, **3**
Borchardt, **15**

Café Oren, **13**
Französischer Hof, **17**
Grossbeerenkeller, **11**
Hardtke, **8**
März, **10**
Paris Bar, **7**

Reinhard's Kurfürstendamm, **4**
Reinhard's Nikolaiviertel, **19**
Rockendorf's, **6**
Thürnagel, **12**
Tucci, **5**
Turmstuben, **16**
VAU, **14**

Zitadellen-Schänke, **1**
Zur Letzten Instanz, **21**
Zur Rippe, **20**

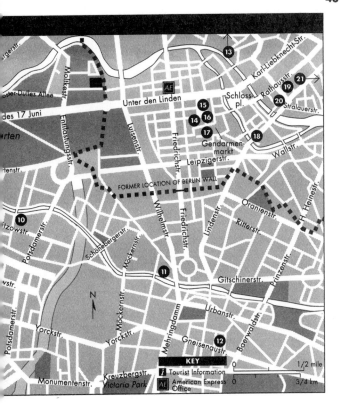

zigerstr.

Molkestr.

ster-Dulles Allee

des 17 Juni

Entlastungsstr.

rten

tenstr.

Unter den Linden

Luisenstr.

Friedrichstr.

Schloss-
pl.

Karl-Liebknecht-Str.

Rathausstr.

13

21

19

20

Stralauerstr.

15

14 **16**

17

Gendarmen-
markt

18

Wallstr.

Leipzigerstr.

FORMER LOCATION OF BERLIN WALL

Wilhelmstr.

Friedrichstr.

Lindenstr.

Oranienstr.

Ritterstr.

H. Heinestr.

10

tzowstr.

Potsdamerstr.

Schöneberger str.

Möckernstr.

vstr.

11

Gitschinerstr.

Prinzenstr.

Baerwaldstr.

N

Möckernstr.

Urbanstr.

Potsdamerstr.

Yorckstr.

Yorckstr.

Mehringdamm

Gneisenaustr.

12

Monumentenstr.

Kreuzbergstr.
Victoria Park

KEY

i Tourist Information

AE American Express
Office

0

1/2 mile

0

3/4 km

room away from the hustle of the bar. The marble walls and striking lighting effects may remind you of a sleek New York restaurant. ⊠ *Schöneberger Ufer 65,* ☎ *030/261–3882. No credit cards. No lunch Sat. or Sun.*

$$ ✕ **Reinhard's.** In the Nikolai Quarter, you'll discover one of eastern Berlin's popular eating establishments. Friends meet here to enjoy the carefully prepared entrées and to sample spirits from the amply stocked bar, all served by friendly, colorful tie-wearing waiters. The honey-glazed breast of duck, *Adlon,* is one of the house specialties. If you just want to hug the bar but find no room here, don't despair; head two doors down to Italian Otello (under the same management). Due to its success, Reinhard's has opened a second restaurant at the Ku'damm. It's much smaller but more elegant and one of the trendiest places in town. Both menu and prices are the same as at Poststrasse. ⊠ *Poststr. 28,* ☎ *030/242–5295;* ⊠ *Kurfürstendamm 190,* ☎ *030/ 881–1621. Reservations essential. AE, DC, MC, V.*

$$ ✕ **Turmstuben.** Not for the infirm or those who are afraid of heights, this restaurant, tucked away below the cupola of the French Cathedral at the north side of the Gendarmenmarkt, is reached by a long, winding staircase. Your reward at the top of the stairs is a table at one of Berlin's most original restaurants. The menu is short, but there's an impressive wine list. ⊠ *Gendarmenmarkt 5,* ☎ *030/ 2044–888. Reservations essential. AE, MC, V.*

$$ ✕ **Zitadellen-Schänke.** Here you'll dine like a medieval noble, served a multicourse menu by Prussian wenches and serenaded by a minstrel group. In winter a roaring fire helps to light and warm the vaulted restaurant, which is part of Spandau's historic Zitadelle. These medieval banquets are popular, so be sure to reserve your spot at one of the heavy, antique oak tables. ⊠ *Am Juliusturm, Spandau,* ☎ *030/334–2106. AE, DC, MC, V. Closed Mon.*

$$ ✕ **Zur Rippe.** This popular eating place in the Nikolai Quarter serves wholesome food in an intimate setting characterized by oak paneling and ceramic tiles. Specialties include the cheese platter and a herring casserole. ⊠ *Poststr. 17,* ☎ *030/242–4248. AE, DC, MC, V.*

$ ✕ **Alt-Cöllner Schankstuben.** A tiny restaurant and pub are contained within this charming, historic Berlin house. The section to the side of the canal on the Kleine Gertraudenstrasse, where there are tables set outside, serves as a café. The menu is relatively limited, but the quality—like the service—is good. ✉ *Friederichsgracht 50, ☎ 030/ 2011–299. Reservations not accepted. AE, DC, MC, V.*

$ ✕ **Blockhaus Nikolskoe.** Prussian king Frederick Wilhelm III built this Russian-style wooden lodge for his daughter Charlotte, wife of Russian czar Nicholas I. South of the city, in Glienecker Park, it offers open-air, riverside dining in summer. Game dishes are prominently featured. ✉ *Nikolskoer Weg 15, ☎ 030/805–2914. DC, MC, V. Closed Thurs.*

$ ✕ **Café Oren.** This popular vegetarian eatery is next to the Neue Synagoge on Oranienburger Strasse, not far from Friedrichstrasse. The restaurant buzzes with loud chatter all evening, and the atmosphere and service are welcoming and friendly. This is the place to enjoy traditional Jewish cooking long absent from the old Jewish quarter of Berlin. Try their *Gefilte fish*, a tasty (and very salty) German-Jewish dish, or *Baichsaibling in schämender butter* (red meat trout in hot butter). The intimate backyard is a wonderful place to enjoy a cool summer evening or a warm autumn afternoon. The extensive menu also offers desserts such as fresh figs filled with mascarpone cheese and served on a fruit sauce and whipped cream. ✉ *Oranienburger Str. 28, ☎ 030/ 282–8228. AE, MC, V.*

$ ✕ **Thürnagel.** The great food served in this vegetarian and seafood restaurant in the Kreuzberg District makes healthful eating fun. The *Tempeh mit Kräutermandelkruste auf Brombeersauce* (soya seeds baked in almonds on blueberry sauce) are good enough to convert a seasoned carnivore. Though the decor is basic, there's linen on the tables and a more upscale atmosphere than you'd expect from a vegetarian's paradise. Take the U-bahn 7 to Südstern to get here. ✉ *Gneisenaustr. 57, ☎ 030/691–4800. MC. No lunch.*

$ ✕ **Zur Letzten Instanz.** Established in 1621, Berlin's old-
★ est restaurant combines the charming atmosphere of old Berlin with a limited (but very tasty) choice of dishes. Napoléon is said to have sat alongside the tile stove in the front room, and Mikhail Gorbachev enjoyed a beer during a visit in 1989. The emphasis here is on beer, both in the recipes and in the mugs. Service can be erratic, though always engagingly friendly. ✉ *Waisenstr. 14–16, ☎ 030/ 242–5528. AE, DC, MC, V.*

4 Lodging

YEAR-ROUND BUSINESS conventions and the influx of summer tourists mean you should make reservations well in advance. If you arrive without reservations, consult hotel boards at airports and train stations, which show hotels with vacancies; or go to the tourist office at Tegel Airport or at the Hauptbahnhof or Zoologischer Garten train stations. The main tourist office in the Europa Center can also help with reservations (☞ Essential Information).

CATEGORY	COST*
$$$$	over DM 350
$$$	DM 270–DM 350
$$	DM 180–DM 270
$	under DM 180

All prices are for two people in a double room, including tax and service.

$$$$ 🏨 **Berlin Hilton.** The Hilton overlooks the historic Gendarmenmarkt and the German and French cathedrals, as well as the classic Schaupielhaus (concert hall). All the right touches are here, from heated bathtubs to special rooms for businesswomen and travelers with disabilities. ⊠ *Mohrenstr. 30, D–10117,* ☎ *030/20230,* 📠 *030/2023–4269. 502 rooms, 42 suites. 4 restaurants, 2 bars, cafeteria, 2 pubs, in-room modem lines, minibars, no-smoking rooms, room service, indoor pool, massage, sauna, exercise room, dance club, baby-sitting, laundry service and dry cleaning, concierge, business services, meeting rooms, parking (fee). AE, DC, MC, V.*

$$$$ 🏨 **Bristol Hotel Kempinski.** Destroyed in the war, rebuilt in 1952, and renovated in 1980, the "Kempi" is a renowned Berlin classic. On the Ku'damm in the heart of the city, it has the best shopping at its doorstep and some fine boutiques of its own within. All rooms and suites are luxuriously decorated and equipped with marble bathrooms, air-conditioning, and cable TV. When you make a reservation, ask for a room in the "superior" category, which will give you all the elegance you'll need at a fair rate. Children under 12 stay for free if they share their parents' room. ⊠ *Kurfürstendamm 27, D–10719,* ☎ *030/884–340,* 📠 *030/883–6075. 301 rooms, 52 suites. 2 restaurants, bar,*

48

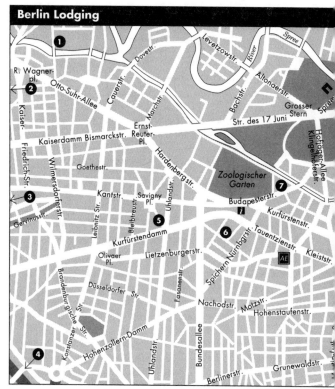

Berlin Lodging

Berlin Hilton, **12**
Bristol Hotel
Kempinski, **5**
Charlottenburger
Hof, **3**
Econtel, **1**
Estrel Residence
Congress
Hotel, **14**

Forum Hotel
Berlin, **13**
Four Seasons
Hotel
Berlin, **11**
Grand Hotel
Esplanade, **8**
Hotel Adlon
Berlin, **9**

Hotel Casino, **2**
Hotel
Müggelsee, **15**
Inter–
Continental
Berlin, **7**
Landhaus
Schlachtensee, **4**

Riehmers
Hofgarten, **16**
Steigenberger
Berlin, **6**
Westin Grand
Hotel, **10**

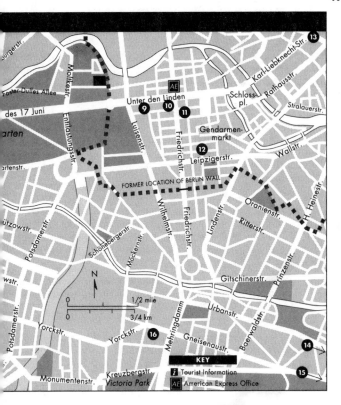

lobby lounge, in-room modem lines, minibars, no-smoking rooms, room service, indoor pool, beauty salon, massage, sauna, exercise room, shops, baby-sitting, laundry service and dry cleaning, concierge, business services, meeting rooms, parking (fee). AE, DC, MC, V.

$$$$ 🏨 **Four Seasons Hotel Berlin.** This latest addition to the cap-
★   ital's hotels combines turn-of-the-century luxury (reminiscent of the *Grand Hotel* of Vicki Baum's novel) with smooth, up-to-date service for the weary business traveler such as portable phones and fax machines. The large guest rooms have all the amenities of a first-class hotel, including free newspapers, overnight dry cleaning, and valet parking. Behind the modern facade of this first-class hotel, thick red carpets, heavy crystal chandeliers, and a romantic restaurant, complete with an open fireplace, help to create a sophisticated and serene atmosphere you thought you never would experience in a bustling city like Berlin. ✉ *Charlottenstr. 49, D–10117,* ☎ *030/20338,* 𝔽𝔸𝕏 *030/2033–6166. 162 rooms, 42 suites. Restaurant, bar, in-room modems, minibars, no-smoking rooms, room service, massage, sauna, exercise room, baby-sitting, laundry service and dry cleaning, concierge, business services, meeting rooms, parking (fee). AE, DC, MC, V.*

$$$$ 🏨 **Grand Hotel Esplanade.** The Grand Hotel Esplanade exudes luxury in its uncompromisingly modern design, its chicly stylish rooms, and the art works by some of Berlin's most acclaimed artists on display. Many rooms on the upper floors have fine panoramic views of the city, though the furnishings, an homage to the cool Bauhaus style, may not be to everybody's taste. You'll appreciate superb facilities and impeccable service. The enormous grand suite comes complete with sauna, whirlpool, and a grand piano—for DM 2,600 per night. ✉ *Lützowufer 15, D–10785,* ☎ *030/254–780,* 𝔽𝔸𝕏 *030/265–1171. 369 rooms, 33 suites. 3 restaurants, bar, lobby lounge, in-room modem lines, minibars, no-smoking rooms, room service, indoor pool, hot tub, sauna, steam room, exercise room, shops, piano, baby-sitting, laundry service and dry cleaning, concierge, business services, convention center, meeting rooms, parking (fee). AE, DC, MC, V.*

$$$$ 🏨 **Hotel Adlon Berlin.** Berlin's premier first-class hotel has
★   to live up to its almost mythical predecessor, the old Hotel

Adlon which, until its destruction during the war, was considered Europe's premier luxury resort, welcoming guests as diverse as Kaiser Wilhelm II and Greta Garbo. The new Adlon is probably the most international hotel in town, both in its impeccable service and with regard to its guest list. When the federal government finally settles into the nearby Reichstag, the Adlon is expected to become its unofficial guesthouse. The lobby is large and light, thanks to its creamy marble and limestone, and a stained-glass cuppola. Businesspeople and visitors curious to see the resurrected hotel sip coffee on the comfortably stuffed chairs and sofas. The dark blue, garnet, and ochre color scheme continues in the guest rooms. All are identically furnished in '20s style with cherry-wood trim, myrtle wood furnishings, and elegant bathrooms in black marble. The more expensive rooms overlook Unter den Linden and the Brandenburger Tor. ⊠ *Unter den Linden 77, D–10117,* ☎ *030/22610,* FAX *030/ 2261–2222. 337 rooms, 51 suites. 2 restaurants, 2 bars, in-room modem lines, in-room safes, minibars, no-smoking floors, room service, indoor pool, beauty salon, massage, sauna, health club, shops, baby-sitting, laundry service and dry cleaning, concierge, business services, meeting rooms, parking (fee). AE, DC, MC, V.*

$$$$ 🖭 **Inter-Continental Berlin.** The rooms and suites in this Berlin classic are all of the highest standard, and their decor shows exquisite taste, with such refinements as luxurious carpets and elegant bathrooms. The west wing offers the best rooms and overlooks the greenery of the vast Tiergarten area. ⊠ *Budapester Str. 2, D–10787,* ☎ *030/26020,* FAX *030/ 2602–80760. 511 rooms, 70 suites. 3 restaurants, bar, in-room modem lines, minibars, no-smoking floors, room service, indoor pool, hot tub, sauna, exercise room, baby-sitting, laundry service and dry cleaning, concierge, business services, convention center, meeting rooms, parking (fee). AE, DC, MC, V.*

$$$$ 🖭 **Steigenberger Berlin.** The Steigenberger group's exemplary Berlin hotel is centrally situated, only a few steps from the Ku'damm, but remarkably quiet. All rooms were re-decorated in 1996 with stylish maple wood furniture. The classy rooms of the new executive club feature late check-in, complimentary ironing and shoe-shine service, a special lounge, and a small breakfast. ⊠ *Los-Angeles-Pl. 1, D–*

10789, ☎ 030/21270, FAX 030/212–7799. 397 rooms, 11 suites. 2 restaurants, café, piano bar, in-room modem lines, in-room-safes, minibars, no-smoking floor, room service, indoor pool, massage, sauna, baby-sitting, laundry service and dry cleaning, concierge, meeting rooms, parking (fee). AE, DC, MC, V.

$$$$ 🏨 **Westin Grand Hotel.** First opened over 10 years ago, this elegant establishment exudes the discreet charm of old money in modern disguise. Since the takeover of former East Berlin's top hotel by the Westin Hotel Group in 1997, the Grand Hotel, located on historic Friedrichstrasse, has undergone a major modernization. The neoclassical pink-marble lobby, with its soaring six-story atrium, has polished brass accents, stucco work, and rich wall coverings. Standard rooms are tastefully decorated in muted tones; bathrooms have large tubs. The service sometimes still lacks a genuine first class approach, but the setting, atmosphere, and architecure of this grand hotel are making it a preferred choice among U.S. travelers. ⊠ *Friedrichstr. 158–164, D–10117, ☎ 030/20270, FAX 030/2027–3362. 323 rooms, 35 suites. 6 restaurants, bar, lobby lounge, in-room modem lines, minibars, no-smoking floors, indoor pool, beauty salon, sauna, exercise room, baby-sitting, laundry service and dry cleaning, concierge, business services, convention center, parking (fee). AE, DC, MC, V.*

$$$ 🏨 **Forum Hotel Berlin.** With its 40 stories, this hotel (owned by Inter-Continental) at the top end of Alexanderplatz competes with the nearby TV tower for the title of premier downtown landmark. As one of the city's largest hotels, it is understandably less personal. Most floors have undergone extensive renovation with fresh carpets and contemporary furniture; when booking, ask for a newly decorated room. Its casino is the highest in Europe and is open until 3 AM. ⊠ *Alexanderpl. 8, D–10178, ☎ 030/23890, FAX 030/2389–4305. 995 rooms, 12 suites. 2 restaurants, bar, in-room modem lines, minibars, no-smoking floors, room service, sauna, exercise room, casino, laundry service and dry cleaning, concierge, business services, parking (fee). AE, DC, MC, V.*

$$ 🏨 **Estrel Residence Congress Hotel.** Europe's biggest hotel may seem huge and anonymous, but it's definitely the only way to get upscale rooms and service for less money. The hotel is located in the unappealing working-class district of Neukölln, some 20 minutes away from the downtown areas. But the modern hotel offers all amenities you can think of and guarantees quiet efficiency and smooth comfort. Rooms are also decorated with Russian art. The lobby hall is a breathtakingly bright atrium, and—thanks to water basins, plants, and huge trees—it has a greenhouse atmosphere. There's also a festival center adjoining the hotel, featuring musicals. ⊠ *Sonnenallee 225, D–12057,* ☎ *030/ 68310,* 𝔽𝔸𝕏 *030/6831–2345. 1,050 rooms, 75 suites. 9 restaurants, bar, lobby lounge, in-room modem lines, minibars, no-smoking floors, indoor pool, beauty salon, sauna, exercise room, concert hall, theater, baby-sitting, children's programs, laundry service and dry cleaning, concierge, business services, convention center, parking (fee). AE, DC, MC, V.*

$$ 🏨 **Hotel Casino.** What were once the main quarters of imperial officers have been skillfully converted into an appealing hotel with large, comfortable rooms, all tastefully furnished and well equipped—the Prussian soldiers never had it so good! The Casino is in the Charlottenburg District. ⊠ *Königen-Elisabeth-Str. 47a, D–14059,* ☎ *030/303– 090,* 𝔽𝔸𝕏 *030/303–0945. 23 rooms. Bar. AE, DC, MC, V.*

$$ 🏨 **Hotel Müggelsee.** Berlin's largest and some say most beautiful lake in the southeastern outskirts of the city is just beyond your balcony at this reliable hotel, which was once a favorite among East Germany's communist leaders. The rooms are not luxurious, but they are renovated, comfortable, and fairly spacious. The hotel can arrange for forest picnics and even has its own yacht for guests' use. ⊠ *Am Grossen Müggelsee, D–12559,* ☎ *030/658–820,* 𝔽𝔸𝕏 *030/ 6588–2263. 174 rooms, 4 apartments. 3 restaurants, bar, no-smoking rooms, massage, sauna, tennis court, health club, boating, bicycles, free parking. AE, DC, MC, V.*

$$ 🏨 **Landhaus Schlachtensee.** Opened in 1987, this former villa (built in 1905) is now a cozy bed-and-breakfast hotel. The Landhaus Schlachtensee offers personal and efficient service, well-equipped rooms, and a quiet location in the Zehlendorf District. The nearby Schlachtensee and Krumme Lanke lakes beckon you to swim, boat, or walk along their shores. ⊠ *Bogotastr. 9, D–14163,* ☎ *030/8099–470,* 𝔽𝔸𝕏 *030/8099– 4747. 20 rooms. Breakfast room, parking (fee). AE, MC, V.*

$$ 🏨 **Riehmers Hofgarten.** The beautifully restored late-19th-
★ century building has high-ceiling rooms that are comfort-
able, with crisp linens and firm beds. A few minutes' walk
from Kreuzberg Hill and the colorful district's restaurants
and bars, and also near Tempelhof Airport, the small hotel
has fast connections to the center of town. ⊠ *Yorckstr. 83,
D–10965,* ☎ *030/781–011,* FAX *030/786–6059. 21 rooms.
Restaurant, bar. AE, DC, MC, V.*

$ 🏨 **Charlottenburger Hof.** A creative flair, convenient loca-
★ tion across from the Charlottenburg S-bahn station, and low
rates make this three-story hotel an incredible value. Kandin-
sky, Miró, and Mondrian are the muses here; their prints
and primary color schemes inspire the rooms and common
spaces. Rooms are individually designed and crafted by the
staff; their variety can suit travelers from friends, to cou-
ples, to families. Whether facing the street or the courtyard,
all rooms receive good light; room amenities include TVs
and hair dryers, but there are no washcloths, and soap dis-
pensers instead of individual soaps. A basic breakfast at the
hotel's 24-hour café is included and the food is good and
healthy, as evidenced by the local patronage. Ironically, the
girly bars in the otherwise residential neighborhhood add
to the safety of the street. Kurfürstendamm is within 10 min-
utes' walking distance, taxis are easy to catch at the S-bahn
station, and the bus to and from Tegel airport stops a block
away. ⊠ *Stuttgarter Platz 14, D–10627,* ☎ *030/32–90–
70,* FAX *030/323–3723. 46 rooms with bath or shower.
Lounge, restaurant, in-room safes, no-smoking rooms, coin
laundry, laundry service, parking (fee). AE, MC, V.*

$ 🏨 **Econtel.** This family-oriented hotel is within walking
distance of Charlottenburg Palace. The spotless rooms
have a homey feel and provide closet safes, cable TV, and
some have a minibar. Families prefer the new family rooms
with four beds, especially decorated for kids. A crib, bot-
tle warmer, and kiddie toilet are available on request free
of charge. The breakfast buffet provides a dazzling array
of choices to fill you up for a day of sightseeing. ⊠ *Söm-
meringstr. 24, D–10589,* ☎ *030/346–810,* FAX *030/3468–
1163. 205 rooms. Bar, in-room safes, no-smoking rooms.
AE, MC, V.*

5 Nightlife and the Arts

TODAY'S BERLIN HAS a tough task living up to the reputation it gained from the film *Cabaret,* but if nightlife has been a little toned down since the '20s and '30s, the arts still flourish. In addition to the many hotels that book seats, there are several ticket agencies, including **Showtime Konzert- und Theaterkassen** (⊠ Tauentzienstr. 21, ☎ 030/217–7754), at the KaDeWe, and Wertheim (⊠ Kurfürstendamm 181, ☎ 030/882–2500), **Theaterkonzertkasse City Center** (⊠ Kurfürstendamm 16, ☎ 030/882–6563), and the **Hek-ticket office** (⊠ Rathausstr. 1 and Kurfürstendamm 14, ☎ 030/2431–2431), at Alexanderplatz, that offer discounted and last-minute tickets. Most of the big stores (Hertie, Wertheim, and Karstadt, for example) also have ticket agencies. Detailed information about what's going on in Berlin can be found in the *Berlin Programm,* a monthly tourist guide to Berlin arts, museums, and theaters; and the magazines *Prinz, tip,* and *zitty,* which appear every two weeks and provide full arts listings. For latest information on Berlin's bustling house, techno, and hip-hop club scene, pick up a copy of *(030),* a free weekly flyer magazine. The only English-language magazine available is *Berlin–the maga-zine,* published four times a year by the city's tourist in-formation office.

THE ARTS

Concerts

Berlin is the home of one of the world's leading orchestras, the **Berliner Philharmonisches Orchester** (☞ Philharmonie, *below*), in addition to a number of other major symphony orchestras and orchestral ensembles. The **Berlin Festival Weeks,** held annually from August through September, combine a wide range of concerts, operas, ballet, theater, and art exhibitions. For information and reservations, write **Festspiele GmbH** (Kartenbüro, ⊠ Budapester Str. 50, D–10787 Berlin, ☎ 030/254–890, FAX 030/2548–9111).

BONUS MILES MAKE GREAT SOUVENIRS.

Calling Card

MCI

123 456 7891 2345
J. D. SMITH

WORLDPHONE

Earn Miles With Your MCI Card.

Take the MCI Card along on this trip and start earning miles for the next one. You'll earn frequent flyer miles on all your calls and save with the low rates you've come to expect from MCI. Before you know it, you'll be on your way to some other international destination.

Sign up for MCI by calling 1-800-FLY-FREE

Earn Frequent Flyer Miles.

Is this a great time, or what? :-)

Easy To Call Home.

1. To use your MCI Card, just dial the WorldPhone access number of the country you're calling from.
2. Dial or give the operator your MCI Card number.
3. Dial or give the number you're calling.

# Austria (CC)★	022-903-012
# Belarus (CC)	
From Brest, Vitebsk, Grodno, Minsk	8-800-103
From Gomel and Mogilev regions	8-10-800-103
# Belgium (CC)♦	0800-10012
# Bulgaria	00800-0001
# Croatia (CC)★	0800-22-0112
# Czech Republic (CC)♦	00-42-000112
# Denmark (CC)♦	8001-0022
# Finland (CC)♦	08001-102-80
# France (CC)♦	0-800-99-0019
# Germany (CC)	0800-888-8000
# Greece (CC)♦	00-800-1211
# Hungary (CC)♦	00▼800-01411
# Iceland (CC)♦	800-9002
# Ireland (CC)	1-800-55-1001
# Italy (CC)♦	172-1022
# Kazakhstan (CC)	8-800-131-4321
# Liechtenstein (CC)♦	0800-89-0222
# Luxembourg	0800-0112
# Monaco (CC)♦	800-90-019
# Netherlands (CC)♦	0800-022-9122
# Norway (CC)♦	800-19912
# Poland (CC)÷	00-800-111-21-22
# Portugal (CC)÷	05-017-1234
Romania (CC)÷	01-800-1800
# Russia (CC)÷ ♦	
To call using ROSTELCOM ■	747-3322
For a Russian-speaking operator	747-3320
To call using SOVINTEL ■	960-2222
# San Marino (CC)♦	172-1022
# Slovak Republic (CC)	00-421-00112
# Slovenia	080-8808
# Spain (CC)	900-99-0014
# Sweden (CC)♦	020-795-922
# Switzerland (CC)♦	0800-89-0222
# Turkey (CC)♦	00-8001-1177
# Ukraine (CC)÷	8▼10-013
# United Kingdom (CC)	
To call using BT ■	0800-89-0222
To call using C&W ■	0500-89-0222
# Vatican City (CC)	172-1022

‡Automation available from most locations. (CC) Country-to-country calling available to/from most international locations. ♦ Public phones may require deposit of coin or phone card for dial tone. ★ Not available from public pay phones. ▼ Wait for second dial tone. ÷ Limited availability. ■ International communications carrier. Limit one bonus program per MCI account. Terms and conditions apply. All airline program rules and conditions apply. © 1998 MCI Telecommunications Corporation. All rights reserved. Is this a great time, or what? is a service mark of MCI.

Concert Halls

Grosser Sendesaal des SFB (⊠ Haus des Rundfunks, Masurenallee 8–14, ☎ 030/303–10). Part of the Sender Freies Berlin, one of Berlin's broadcasting stations, the Grosser Sendesaal is the home of the Radio Symphonic Orchestra.

Konzerthaus Berlin (⊠ In the Schauspielhaus; Gendarmenmarkt, ☎ 030/2030–92101). This beautifully restored hall is a prime venue for concerts in historic Berlin.

Konzertsaal der Hochschule der Künste (⊠ Hardenbergstr. 33, ☎ 030/3185–2374). The concert hall of the Academy of Fine Arts is Berlin's second largest.

Philharmonie mit Kammermusiksaal (⊠ Matthäikircherstr. 1, ☎ 030/254–880 or 030/2548–8132). The Berlin Philharmonic is based here. The adjoining hall houses the smaller Kammermusiksaal, dedicated to chamber music.

Waldbühne (⊠ Am Glockenturm, close to the Olympic Stadium, ☎ 030/305–5079). Modeled after an ancient Roman theater, this open-air site accommodates nearly 20,000 people.

Dance, Musicals, and Opera

Despite dramatic cutbacks in the city's budget for culture, Berlin still clings to its three **opera houses**, all of which have their own ballet companies: the **Deutsche Oper Berlin** (⊠ Bismarckstr. 34–37, ☎ 030/343–8401); the **Staatsoper Unter den Linden** (⊠ Unter den Linden 7, ☎ 030/2035–4555), Germany's leading opera house; and the **Komische Oper** (⊠ Behrenstr. 55–57, ☎ 030/4702–1000 or 01805/304168), which often has modern dance productions by international choreographers. The **Neuköllner Oper** (⊠ Karl-Marx-Str. 131–133, ☎ 030/6889–0777) has showy, fun performances of long-forgotten operas as well as humorous musical productions.

For **comic operas and musicals,** such as *West Side Story, Shakespeare & Rock'n'Roll, A Chorus Line,* and *Cabaret,* head for **Estrel Festival Center** (⊠ Sonnenallee 225/Ziegrastr. 21–29, ☎ 030/6831–6831); **Theater des Westens** (⊠ Kantstr. 12, ☎ 030/882–2888), Germany's leading musical theater;

the **Metropol Theater** (✉ Friedrichstr. 101, ☎ 030/2024–6117); the **Schiller-Theater** (✉ Bismarckstr. 110, ☎ 030/3111–3111); and the **Space Dream Musical Theater** (✉ Tempelhof Airport, Clumbiadamm 2–6, ☎ 030/6951–2802).

Please note: Berlin's largest musical theater is likely to open in 1999 at the Potsdamer Platz Arkaden. At press time, however, details were unavailable. Contact one of Berlin's tourist information offices for further details.

Experimental and modern-dance performances are presented at **Podewil** (✉ Klosterstr. 68–70, ☎ 030/247–496), **Tanzfabrik** (✉ Möckernstr. 68, ☎ 030/786–5861), and the **Theater am Halleschen Ufer** (☞ *below*).

Film

Berlin has about 110 movie theaters, showing about 100 films a day. International and German movies are shown in the big theaters around the Ku'damm; the off-Ku'damm theaters show less-commercial movies. For (undubbed) movies in English, go to the **Babylon** (✉ Dresdnerstr. 126, ☎ 030/614–6316), the **Kurbel** (✉ Giesebrechtstr. 4, ☎ 030/883–5325), or the **Odeon** (✉ Hauptstr. 116, ☎ 030/781–5667).

In February, Berlin hosts the **Internationale Filmfestspiele,** an internationally famous film festival, conferring the Golden Bear award on the best films, directors, and actors. Call 030/254–890 for information.

Theater

Theater in Berlin is outstanding, but performances are usually in German. The exceptions are operettas and the (nonliterary) cabarets. Of the city's impressive number of theaters, the most renowned for both their **modern and classical productions** are the **Schaubühne am Lehniner Platz** (✉ Kurfürstendamm 153, ☎ 030/890–023) and the **Deutsches Theater** (✉ Schumannstr. 13, ☎ 030/284–41225), which has an excellent studio theater next door, the **Kammerspiele** (☎ 030/284–41226).

The **Berliner Ensemble** (✉ Bertolt Brecht-Pl. 1, ☎ 030/282–3160) is dedicated to Brecht and works of other interna-

tional playwrights. The **Hebbel Theater** (✉ Stresemannstr. 29, ☎ 030/259–0040) showcases international theater and dance troupes. The **Maxim Gorki Theater** (✉ Am Festungsgraben 2, ☎ 030/2022–1115) also has a superb studio theater. The **Volksbühne am Rosa-Luxemburg-Platz** (✉ Rosa-Luxemburg-Pl., ☎ 030/247–6772 or 030/24065661) is known for its radical interpretations of dramas. For **boulevard plays** (fashionable social comedies), try the **Hansa Theater** (✉ Alt-Moabit 48, ☎ 030/391–4460), the **Komödie** (✉ Kurfürstendamm 206, ☎ 030/4702–1010), and, at the same address, the **Theater am Kurfürstendamm** (☎ 030/4702–1010 or 030/882–3789).

For smaller, more **alternative theaters**, which generally showcase different guest productions, try **Theater am Halleschen Ufer** (✉ Hallesches Ufer 32, ☎ 030/651–0655), or **Theater Zerbrochene Fenster** (✉ Fidicinstr. 3, ☎ 030/694–2400).

Social and political satire has a long tradition in cabaret theaters here. The **Stachelschweine** (✉ Europa Center, ☎ 030/261–4795) and **Die Wühlmäuse** (✉ Nürnbergerstr. 33, ☎ 030/213–7047) carry on that tradition with biting wit and style. Eastern Berlin's equivalents are the **Distel** (✉ Friedrichstr. 101, ☎ 030/204–4704) and **Kartoon** (✉ Französische Str. 24, ☎ 030/2044–756). For **children's theater**, head for the world-famous **Grips Theater** (✉ Altonaer Str. 22, ☎ 030/391–4004) or **Hans Wurst Nachfahren** (✉ Gleditschstr. 5, ☎ 030/216–7925). Both are nominally for children but can be good entertainment for adults as well.

For English-language theater try the **Friends of Italian Opera** (✉ Fidicinstr. 40, ☎ 030/6911211), presenting both classical British and American drama as well as modern productions.

Variety Shows

During the past few years Berlin has become Germany's prime hot spot for variety shows, presenting magic, artistic, and circus performances, sometimes combined with music and classic cabaret. The world's largest variety show is presented at the **Friedrichstadtpalast** (✉ Friedrichstr. 107,

☎ 030/2326–2474), a glossy showcase for revues, famous for its female dancers. The **Wintergarten** (✉ Potsdamer Str. 96, ☎ 030/2308–8230 or 030/2500–8863) pays romantic homage to the old days of Berlin's original variety theater in the '20s. Intimate and intellectually entertaining is the **Bar jeder Vernunft** (✉ Spiegelzelt, Schaperstr. 24, ☎ 030/8831–582), whose name is a pun, literally meaning "devoid of any reason." The **Chamäleon Varieté** (✉ Rosenthaler Str. 40/41, ☎ 030/2827–118) has risen to near stardom in the city's off-scene thanks to its extremely funny shows featuring acrobats, comedians, and oddly talented entertainers. Very little knowledge of German is necessary to get all the gags. It's located within Hackesche Höfe, an art nouveau courtyard with some trendy bars for pre- or after-show drinks.

NIGHTLIFE

Bars

The bars here are distinguished from the Kneipen listed further below by the prices of drinks and the upscale dress code.

Bar am Lützowplatz (✉ Am Lützowpl. 7, ☎ 030/2626–807). A Berlin classic, this fancy bar with the longest counter in town is a must for nighthawks. The bar attracts some of the town's most beautiful women, who enjoy American cocktails while flirting with the handsome bartenders.

Champussy (✉ Uhlandstr. 171–172, ☎ 030/8812–220). At this elegant spot, bartenders devote all their knowledge to serving the best champagne cocktails in town. The interior is definitely first class, with the bar hidden behind massive white columns.

Harry's New York Bar (✉ Am Lützowufer 15, ☎ 030/2547–8821). This is probably the best hotel bar in town, situated in the lobby of Berlin's Grand Hotel Esplanade. It's also one of the few in the city that features live piano music. Businessmen try to relax under the portraits of American presidents and modern paintings hanging on the wall.

Casinos

Spielbank Berlin (✉ Europa Center, ☎ 030/2500–890).
Berlin's leading casino with 10 roulette tables and 3 black-jack tables stays open 3 PM–3 AM. The **Casino Berlin** is less
fashionable and international but is worth a visit for its
breathtaking location on top of the Forum Hotel at Alexan-derplatz (✉ Alexanderplatz, ☎ 030/2389–4113).

Gay Nightlife

Berlin is unmistakably Germany's gay capital, and many
visitors from other European countries also come to par-take of the city's gay scene. Concentrated in Schöneberg
(around Nollendorfplatz) and Kreuzberg, and growing in
Mitte and Prenzlauer Berg in eastern Berlin, the scene of-fers great diversity.

The following places are a good starting point for infor-mation. Also check out the magazines *Siegessäule, (030),*
and *Sergej* (free and available at the places listed below as
well as many others around town).

Mann-O-Meter (✉ Motzstr. 5, ☎ 030/216–8008). You
can get extensive information about gay life, groups, and
events. Talks are held in the café, which has a variety of
books and magazines. Open Monday–Friday 3–11, Sat-urday 3–10.

Schwuz (✉ Mehringdamm 61, ☎ 030/694–1077). This gay
gathering spot sponsors different events. Every Saturday
starting at 11 PM there is an "open evening" for talk and
dance.

Kneipen

Anderes Ufer (✉ Hauptstr. 157, ☎ 030/7841–578). A
young gay and lesbian crowd frequents this hip Kneipe. It
has a mellow atmosphere and '50s and '60s music.

Hafenbar (✉ Motzstr. 18, ☎ 030/2114–118). The interior
and the energetic crowd make this gay bar endlessly pop-ular and a favorite singles place. At 4 AM people move next
door to Tom's Bar, open until 6 AM.

Discos

Connection (⌧ Welserstr. 24, ☎ 030/2181–432). Close to Wittenbergplatz, this disco offers heavy house music and lots of dark corners. It's open Friday and Saturday, midnight until 6.

Schwuz (☞ *Above*).

Kneipen

The city's roughly 6,000 bars and pubs all come under the heading of *Kneipen*—the place around the corner where you stop in for a beer, a snack, and conversation—and sometimes to dance. Other than along Ku'damm and its side streets, the happening places in western Berlin are around **Savignyplatz** in Charlottenburg, **Nollendorfplatz** and **Winterfeldplatz** in Schöneberg, **Ludwigkirchplatz** in Wilmersdorf, and along **Oranienstrasse** and **Wienerstrasse** in Kreuzberg. In eastern Berlin most of the action is along **Oranienburger Strasse**: north in Mitte; its surrounding streets to the northeast; the **Rosenthaler Platz**, with the impressive and always bustling **Hackesche Höfe**; and also around **Kollwitzplatz**, in Prenzlauer Berg.

Green Door (⌧ Winterfeldstr. 50, ☎ 030/2152–515). At this Schöneberg classic, at the location of Berlin's legendary Havanna Bar, the city's hip crowd gets together for a drink. Don't try this place if you are not into alternative and wild fashion. The cocktails are outstanding, though.

Hackbarths (⌧ Augustr. 49a, ☎ 030/282–7706). This is only one of many similar alternative bars and clubs, mostly frequented by students in the Oranienburger Strasse neighborhood.

Kumpelnest 3000 (⌧ Lützowstr. 23, ☎ 030/2616–918). After you've been here, you might argue about whether or not this place is really a bar. It's a hot spot for kinky nightclubbers only, where a crowd of both gays and heteros mingle. Nobody really cares about the quality of the drinks, although the beer is good.

Leydicke (✉ Mansteinstr. 4, ☎ 030/2162–973). This historic spot is a must for out-of-towners. The proprietors operate their own distillery and have a superb selection of sweet wines and liqueurs.

Silberstein (✉ Oranienburger Str. 27, ☎ 030/2812–095). You might pass this place up at first, mistaking it for an art gallery, and you wouldn't be entirely wrong—it's that *and* also one of the city's trendiest meeting places.

Jazz Clubs

Berlin's lively music scene is dominated by jazz and rock. For jazz enthusiasts *the* events of the year are the summer's **Jazz in the Garden** festival and the autumn international **Jazz Fest Berlin.** For information, call the tourist information center (☎ 030/262–6031).

A-Trane Jazzclub (✉ Pestalozzistr. 105, ☎ 030/313–2550). A stylish newcomer, the A-Trane has found its fans among Berlin's jazz community. The club has studiolike equipment and is often used for radio recordings.

Eierschale (I) (✉ Podbielskiallee 50, ☎ 030/832–7097). A variety of jazz groups appears here at the "Egg Shell," one of Berlin's oldest jazz clubs, open daily from 8:30 PM. Admission is free.

Flöz (✉ Nassauische Str. 37, ☎ 030/861–1000). The sizzling jazz at this club sometimes accompanies theater presentations.

Knaack-Club (✉ Greifswalder 224, ☎ 030/442–7060). This eastern Berlin club brings in jazz and rock'n'roll names and often follows up the acts with hours of dancing.

Quasimodo (✉ Kantstr. 12a, ☎ 030/312–8086). The most established and popular jazz venue in the city has a great basement atmosphere and a good seating arrangement.

Nightclubs

Though it's a day-and-night event, it seems best to mention this orgiastic event under this category: **The Love Pa-**

rade. Every July, hundreds of thousands of European ravers spill out of trains to attend Berlin's Love Parade—a zany, outdoor, free-for-all celebration of techno music and its culture. If you want to be part of it, start planning your costume now. Contact the tourist office (☞ Essential Information) for the exact dates.

Blue Note (✉ Courbierestr. 13, ☎ 030/3141–237). Here's an intimate bar with a tiny disco floor where the beautiful dance the night away. The cocktails are delicious, the music is no-nonsense soul and funk, and most guests are older than 30.

Far Out (✉ Kurfürstendamm 156, ☎ 030/320–007). This formerly Bhagwan-operated disco has the cleanest air in the city and one of the biggest dance floors, where the mostly young crowd—in their early twenties—enjoys mostly old hits. Tuesday is no-smoking night; closed Monday.

90 Grad (✉ Dennewitzstr. 37, ☎ 030/2628–984). This jam-packed disco plays hip-hop, soul, and some techno and really gets going around 2 AM. Women come fashionably dressed and go right in, but men usually have to wait outside until they get picked by the doorman.

Sophienklub (✉ Sophienstr. 6, ☎ 030/2824–552). A gathering spot for mostly local former East Berliners, this cramped disco always serves up a formidable music mix. It's heavy on acid jazz. The bars of Hackesche Höfe and Chamäleon Varieté are just around the corner.

6 Outdoor Activities and Sports

BERLIN HAS MORE SPORTS activities to participate in rather than to watch. Swimming at one of the lakes or biking throughout the city is both easy to arrange and provides beautiful views of the city.

Biking

There are bike paths throughout the downtown area and the rest of the city. Call the **Allgemeiner Deutscher Fahrrad-Club, ADFC** (⌧ Brunnenstr. 28, ☎ 030/4484–724) for information and rental locations, or rent your bikes at some of the major hotels for approximately DM 30 for 24 hours. **Bikecity** (⌧ Pohlstrasse 89, near corner of Kluckstrasse, U-bahn Kurfürstenstrasse, ☎ 030/2655–0403) also has a social agenda of providing job training to youth and senior citizens. A passport must be left for security on the green rental bikes. Call for their other locations. **Fahrrad Vermietung Berlin** (☎ 030/261–2094) rents black bikes with baskets, which they keep at a lamppost at the corner of the Europa Center on Tauentzienstrasse. Money-wise, bikes are rented by the day (not 24 hours), and you must leave either a DM200 deposit or your passport as security. If someone isn't there, just wait, or see if there is a sky-blue bus parked nearby. The person is probably signing up a bus tour there and will return shortly.

Golf

Berlin's leading club is the **Golf- und Land Club Berlin-Wannsee** (⌧ Am Stölpchenweg, Wannsee, ☎ 030/806–7060).

Horseback Riding

Horses can be rented at the **Reitsportschule Onkel Toms Hütte** (⌧ Onkel-Tom-Str. 172, ☎ 030/8132–081), **Reitschule Stall-Schmitz** (⌧ Hennigsdorfer Str. 162, Berlin-Heiligensee, ☎ 030/4319–393), and **Reitsportschule Haflinger Hof** (⌧ Feldweg 21, Fredersdorf, close to Berlin, ☎ 033439/6371).

Jogging

The **Tiergarten** is the best place for jogging in the downtown area. Run its length and back and you'll have covered 8 km (5 mi). Joggers can also take advantage of the grounds of **Schloss Charlottenburg,** 3 km (2 mi) around. For longer runs, anything up to 32 km (20 mi), make for the **Grunewald.** In general, all of these woods are safe. You should, however, avoid Grunewald and Tiergarten during dark winter evenings.

Sailing and Windsurfing

Boats and boards of all kinds are rented by **Albrecht Wassersport** (⊠ Kaiserdamm 95, ☎ 030/3007–464).

Squash and Tennis

There are tennis courts and squash centers throughout the city; ask your hotel to direct you to the nearest of these. **Tennis & Squash City** (⊠ Brandenburgische Str. 53, Wilmersdorf, ☎ 030/8739–097) has 6 tennis courts and 11 squash courts. At **Tennisplätze am Ku'damm** (⊠ Cicerostr. 55A, ☎ 030/891–6630), you can step right off the Ku'damm and onto a tennis court.

Swimming

The **Wannsee,** the **Halensee,** and the **Plötzensee** all have beaches; they get crowded during summer weekends, however. There are public pools throughout the city, so there's bound to be at least one near where you're staying. For full listings ask at the tourist office. Berlin's most impressive pool is the **Olympia-Schwimmstadion** at Olympischer Platz (U-bahn: Olympiastadion).The **Blub Badeparadies** lido (⊠ Buschkrugallee 64, ☎ 030/606–6060) has indoor and outdoor pools, a sauna garden, hot whirlpools, and a solarium (U-bahn: Grenzallee).

7 Shopping

THERE ARE PLENTY OF souveneir items in Berlin to bring home with you: beer steins, ceramics, wood handcrafts, chocolates, and even Russian army momentos or reproductions. Though the exchange rate is in the dollar's favor, fine clothing and shoe prices are generally higher in Berlin than in U.S. cities.

Shopping Districts

Charlottenburg

For trendier clothes, try the boutiques along the side streets of the Ku'damm, such as Fasanenstrasse, Knesebeckstrasse, Mommsenstrasse, Bleibtreustrasse, Schlüterstrasse, and Uhlandstrasse. Less trendy and much less expensive is the outdoor shopping mall along **Wilmersdorfer Strasse** (U-7 station of same name), where price-conscious Berliners do their shopping. It's packed on weekends.

Friedrichstrasse

This rebuilt boulevard offers the most elegant shops in historic Berlin, including a new **Galeries Lafayette** department store. Nearby Unter den Linden has a mix of expensive boutiques, particularly between Friedrichstrasse and the Brandenburger Tor. These include a Meissen ceramic showroom, a store that sells old costumes from one of the opera houses, and tourist souvenir shops—some with well-crafted wooden toys, ornaments, and figurines. Around **Alexanderplatz,** more affordable stores offer everything from clothes to electronic goods to designer perfumes. Many smaller clothing and specialty stores have sprung up in and around the **Nikolai Quarter.**

Kurfürstendamm

The city's liveliest and most famous shopping area is still found around Kurfürstendamm and its side streets, especially between **Breitscheidplatz** and **Olivaer Platz.** The **Europa Center** (☎ 030/348–0088) at Breitscheidplatz encompasses more than 100 stores, cafés, and restaurants—although this is not the place to hunt for bargains. Running east from Breitscheidplatz is **Tauentzienstrasse,** another shopping street. At the end of it is Berlin's most celebrated department store, the **Kaufhaus des Westens** or KaDeWe.

The elegant **Uhland-Passage** (⊠ 170 Uhlandstr.) has leading name stores as well as cafés and restaurants. The new
Kempinski Plaza (⊠ Uhlandstr. 181–183) features exclusive boutiques and a pleasant atrium café.

Potsdamer Platz Arkaden

The city's newest shopping mall on Potsdamer Platz is also
its fanciest. More than 150 upscale and international shops,
cafés, and restaurants under high glass ceilings and marble columns make this a shopper's paradise in the historic
heart of Berlin.

Department Stores

Galeries Lafayette (⊠ Französische Str. 23, ☎ 030/209–
480). This intimate and elegant counterpart to the KaDeWe
has evolved as the city's most popular department store.
Only a sixth of the KaDeWe's size, it carries almost exclusively French products, including designer clothes, perfume, and all the French produce you might need for
preparing your own *haute cuisine* at home.

Kaufhaus des Westens (KaDeWe) (⊠ Tauentzienstr. 21, ☎
030/21210). The largest department store in Europe, with
more than 68,000 square m (733,000 square ft) even sur-
passing London's Harrods, the undeniably classy KaDeWe
has undergone a complete redesign. It has a grand selection of goods on seven floors, as well as food and deli
counters, champagne bars, restaurants, and beer bars on
its two upper floors.

Kaufhof (⊠ Alexanderpl., ☎ 030/247430). Situated at the
north end of Alexanderplatz, the Kaufhof is worth a visit
for its stunning gourmet food department.

Wertheim (⊠ Kurfürstendamm 181, ☎ 030/8800–3206).
The other main department store downtown is neither as
big nor as attractive as the KaDeWe, but Wertheim nonetheless offers a large selection of fine wares.

Gift Shops

Berlin is a city of alluring stores and boutiques. Despite its
cosmopolitan gloss, shop prices are generally lower than

in cities like Munich and Hamburg. Most stores offer tax-free shopping for non-European Union citizens, so be sure to ask about it before making your purchase.

For inexpensive gifts for yourself and loved ones left at home, German (and also Swiss) chocolates are a hit with any sweet tooth. Department stores and most supermarkets carry a wide selection, from chocolate bars by Sarotti, Milka, and Ritter Sport, to Lindt truffle assortments and marzipan (made with almond paste) confections.

Bürgel-Haus (⊠ Friedrichstrasse 154, ☎ 030/2045–2695) carries the Blaudruck ceramic tablewear that is crafted in the eastern state of Thuringia, just south of Berlin. Serving dishes, cups, coffeepots and the like are painted a solid bright blue with white polka dot accents. The simple, cheerful style actually goes well with American country kitchens. The store is open Monday through Saturday, 9–6.

Gipsformerei der Staatlichen Museen Preussischer Kulturbesitz (⊠ Sophie-Charlotte-Str. 17, ☎ 030/321–7011). If you long to have the Egyptian Museum's Queen Nefertiti bust on your mantelpiece at home (the original is at the Ägyptisches Museum; ☞ Chapter 2), check out the state museum's shop, open weekdays 9–4, which sells plaster casts of treasures from the city's museums.

Königliche Porzellan Manufaktur. Fine porcelain is still produced by this former Royal Prussian Porcelain Factory, also called KPM. You can buy this delicate handmade, hand-painted china at KPM's store (⊠ Kurfürstendamm 26A, ☎ 030/8867–210), but it may be more fun to visit the factory salesroom (⊠ Wegelystr. 1, ☎ 030/390–090), which also sells seconds at reduced prices.

Specialty Stores

Antiques

Not far from Wittenbergplatz lies Keithstrasse, a street full of antiques stores. Eisenacher Strasse, Fuggerstrasse, Kalckreuthstrasse, Motzstrasse, and Nollendorfstrasse—all close to Nollendorfplatz—have many antiques stores of varying quality. Another good street for antiques is Suarezstrasse, between Kantstrasse and Bismarckstrasse.

Berliner Antik- und Flohmarkt. This is one of the largest, more established, and expensive places dealing in antique art. It offers everything from costly antique lamps to bargain books. Many antiques stores are found under the tracks at the Friedrichstrasse station (☎ 030/208–2645), open Monday and Wednesday–Sunday 11–6.

Berliner Kunstmarkt (Berlin Art Market). On Saturday and Sunday from 10 to 5, the colorful and lively antiques and handicrafts fair on **Strasse des 17. Juni** swings into action. Don't expect to pick up many bargains—or to have the place to yourself.

Christie's (⊠ Fasanenstr. 72, ☎ 030/881–4164). The venerable auction house has an outpost just off the Ku'damm.

Sotheby's (⊠ Palais am Festungsgraben on Unter den Linden, ☎ 030/204–4119). The international auction house has set up shop in one of historic Berlin's more beautiful buildings, staging auctions on a regular basis.

English-Language Bookstores
Although we specifically list bookstores that carry English books here, take the time to browse through any bookstore you come across. Among the plethora of fine art, architecture, antique, and coffee-table books, you'll see a graphic-design quality that is often much more bold than in the States.

Books in Berlin (⊠ Goethestr. 69, Charlottenburg, ☎ 030/313–1233). **British Bookshop** (⊠ Mauerstr. 82–84, ☎ 030/238–4680). **Marga Schoeller Bücherstube** (⊠ Knesebeckstr. 33, ☎ 030/881–1112). **Buchhandlung Kiepert** (⊠ Hardenbergstr. 4–5, ☎ 030/311–0090). **Hugendubel** (⊠ Tauentzienstr. 13, ☎ 030/214060). **Dussmann Kulturkaufhaus** (⊠ Friedrichstr. 90, ☎ 030/20250).

Hats
Chapeaux (⊠ Bleibtreustrasse 4, ☎ 030/312–0913) is run by milliner Andrea Cutti, whose self-made hats for men and women share the boutique with the clothing and accessories of designer Setareh Makinejad. Hats, which range from day- to wedding- to evening-wear are DM250 to DM500; jewelry is from DM50 to DM250.

Jewelry

Axel Sedlatzek (⊠ Kurfürstendamm 45, ☎ 030/881–1627), a Berlin classic, is one of the largest jewelers in town.

Bucherer (⊠ Kurfürstendamm 26a, ☎ 030/8804–030), one of Berlin's new and upscale jewelers, carries fine hand-crafted jewelry, watches, and other stylish designer products.

Rio (⊠ Bleibtreustrasse 52, ☎ 030/3133–152) carries fun but tasteful costume jewelry, mostly by designer Barbara Kranz, but also by some Brits. Much of the selection of ear-rings, bracelets, and necklaces features luminous, colorful frosted glass set in bright silver; other necklaces and ear-rings mimic antique styles. No one offers more, or more attractive clip-on earrings. The hat store (☞ **Chapeaux**, *above*) is across the street.

Men's Clothing

Budapester Schuhe (⊠ Kurfürstendamm 199, ☎ 030/881–1707). A Berlin classic, this old-style shop for men's shoes offers the largest selection of business shoes in all designs and colors.

Mientus (⊠ Wilmersdorfer Str. 73, ⊠ Kurfürstendamm 52, ☎ 030/323–9077 for both). This large, exclusive men's store caters to expensive tastes. It offers both conventional and business wear, as well as sporty and modern looks, and carries many top designer labels.

Selbach (⊠ Kurfürstendamm 195/196, ☎ 030/262–7038). Come here for elegant evening clothes and fashionable de-signer labels for the young crowd—at a high price.

Women's Clothing

Bogner-Shop Zenker (⊠ Kurfürstendamm 45, ☎ 030/881–1000). For German designer wear, try this boutique. It's not cheap, but the styling is classic.

Granny's Step (⊠ Kurfürstendamm 56, ☎ 030/323–7660). Next to Kramberg you'll find evening wear styled along the lines of bygone times.

Kramberg (⊠ Kurfürstendamm 56, ☎ 030/327–9010). If you're looking for international labels, including Gucci, Ar-mani, and Chanel, drop by here and enjoy the first-class atmosphere in this top-of-the-world store.

Nouvelle (⊠ Bleibtreustr. 24, ☎ 030/881–4737). Browse through this extraordinary lingerie store if you're feeling daring. Elegant '20s intimate wear made of fine, old-fashioned materials is its specialty.

Peek und Cloppenburg (⊠ Tauentzienstr. 19, ☎ 030/212–900). Europe's second-largest clothing store, affectionately called "P and C," offers women's, men's, and children's wear on five floors. A special *Joop!* designer store on the top floor and the international designer department in the basement should not be missed.

Toys
Klein-Holz (⊠ Belziger Strasse 26, U-bahn Eisenacher Str., ☎ 030/781–1088, ⊠ Stuttgarter Platz 21, U-bahn Charlottenburg, ☎ 030/323–8681) sells books and wooden toys for kids up to 8 years old. Most of the toys are made in Germany and England; proceeds of the profits support an anti-drug program for youth.

8 Side Trips from Berlin

A **TRIP TO BERLIN** wouldn't be complete without paying a visit to Brandenburg, the rural state that surrounds the city. Even if you have only a few days left, you should spare a day or two for visiting it. In contrast to Berlin's vibrant urbanity, Brandenburg's lovely countryside is a pleasant surprise, with green meadows to the north and pine barrens to the east and south. Sightseeing highlights include the 18th-century palace of Sanssouci, near Potsdam, the old capital of Brandenburg; and Frankfurt an der Oder, a frontierlike small town at the German-Polish border.

POTSDAM

Prussia's most famous king, Friedrich II—Frederick the Great—spent more time at his summer residence, **Sanssouci** in Potsdam, than at the official court in Berlin, and it's no wonder. Frederick was an aesthetic ruler, and he clearly fell for the sheer beauty of the sleepy township lost among the hills, meadows, and lakes of this rural corner of mighty Prussia. Sanssouci is contained in a beautifully landscaped park. Its name means "without a care" in French, the language Frederick tried to cultivate in his own private circle and within the court. Some experts believe Frederick actually named the palace "Sans, Souci," which they translate as "with and without a care," a more apt name; its construction caused him a lot of trouble and expense and sparked furious rows with his master builder, Georg Wenzeslaus von Knobelsdorff. His creation nevertheless became one of Germany's greatest tourist attractions—5 million visitors a year file through the palace and grounds.

Frederick wanted to be buried, with no pomp and circumstance, beside his hunting dogs on the terrace of his beloved Sanssouci; a "philosopher's funeral" was what he decreed. His shocked nephew and successor, Friedrich Wilhelm II, ordered the body to be laid out in state and then consigned Frederick's remains to the garrison church of Potsdam. The coffin was removed to safety during World War II, after which it went on a macabre peregrination that ended in the chapel of the Hohenzollern Castle in southern Germany. The unification of Germany in 1991 made it possible to grant Frederick his last wish.

Executed according to Frederick's impeccable French-influenced taste, the palace, built from 1745 to 1747, is extravagantly rococo, with scarcely a patch of wall left unadorned. To the west of the palace is the **New Chambers** (1747), which housed guests of the king's family; originally it functioned as a greenhouse until it was remodeled in 1771–74. Just east of Sanssouci Palace is the **Bildergalerie** (Picture Gallery) (1755–63), reopened three years ago. After extensive renovation, the building was given back its original look, including expensive marble from Siena in the main cupola. The gallery displays Frederick's collection of 17th-century Italian and Dutch paintings, including works by Caravaggio, Rubens, and van Dyck. *Sanssouci Central Visitor Information:* ☎ *0331/969–4202 or 0331/969–4203/204 (tape with opening hrs and current entrance fees).* ✉ *Besucherzentrum an der Historischen Mühle.* ⟡ *Apr.–Oct., daily 8:30–5; Nov.–Mar., daily 9–4.* ▣ *DM 20 for a special ticket pass, valid for one day and all buildings and museums in Sanssouci and Potsdam. Palace of Sanssouci:* ☎ *0331/969–4190.* ▣ *Guided tour DM 10.* ⟡ *Apr.–Oct., Tues.–Sun. 9–5, Nov.– Mar., Tues.–Sun. 9–4. New Chambers:* ☎ *0331/969–4206.* ▣ *Guided tour DM 5.* ⟡ *Apr.–Oct., Tues.–Sun. 10–5. Picture Gallery:* ☎ *0331/969–4181.* ▣ *DM 4.* ⟡ *May–Oct., Tues.–Sun. 10–5.*

Neues Palais (New Palace), a much larger and grander palace than Sanssouci, stands at the end of the long straight avenue that runs through Sanssouci Park. It was built after the Seven Years' War (1756–63), when Frederick loosened the purse strings. It's said he wanted to demonstrate to his subjects that the state coffers hadn't been depleted too severely by the long conflict. Frederick rarely stayed here, however, preferring the relative coziness of Sanssouci. Still, the Neues Palais has much of interest, including an indoor grotto hall, an extravaganza out of a Jules Verne novel, with walls and columns set with shells, coral, and other aquatic decoration. The upper gallery contains paintings by 17th-century Italian masters and a bijou court theater in which drama and opera performances are still given. Tickets for the Neues Palais theater

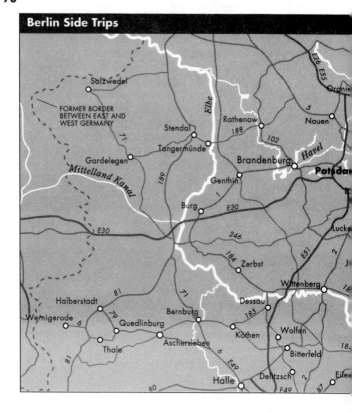

Berlin Side Trips

Salzwedel

FORMER BORDER
BETWEEN EAST AND
WEST GERMANY

71

Gardelegen

Mittelland Kanal

Stendal

Tangermünde

189

Elbe

Rathenow

188

102

Havel

Brandenburg

Genthin

1

Burg

E30

E30

246

184 Zerbst

Oranie

5

Nauen

Potsda

Lucke

E51

2

J

Wittenberg

18

Halberstadt

81

79

Wernigerode

6

Quedlinburg

Thale

81

Bernburg

Aschersleben

6

Dessau

185

Köthen

Wolfen

Bitterfeld

E49

18.

Halle

80

Delitzsch

2

F49

87

Eiler

Eberswalde

167

E28

2

Bad
Freienwalde

167

Bernau

E55

erlin

5

Rüdersdorf

**Frankfurt
an der Oder**

Fürstenwalde

E30

Königs
Wusterhausen

Oder

POLAND

E55

elde

246

Eisenhüttenstadt

112

101

96

E36-E55

87

Guben

97

Lübben

Lübbenau

115 Cottbus

Forst

102

E36

87

115

96

101

E55

Senftenberg

Lauchhammer

Hoyerswerda

156

Schwarzheide

115

Elsterwerda

97

96

0   30 miles

0   45 km

N

GERMANY

are sold at the Potsdam Information (☞ Visitor Information, *below*). ⊠ *Strasse am Neuen Palais,* ☎ *0331/969–4255.* ✉ *DM 8, including guided tour.* ⊙ *Apr.–Oct., Sat.–Thurs. 9–5; Nov.–Mar., Sat.–Thurs. 9–4.*

Schloss Charlottenhof stands on its own grounds in the southern part of Sanssouci Park. After Frederick died in 1786, the ambitious Sanssouci building program ground to a halt, and the park fell into neglect. It was 50 years before another Prussian king, Frederick William III, restored Sanssouci's earlier glory. He engaged the great Berlin architect Karl Friedrich Schinkel to build a small palace for the crown prince, Schloss Charlottenhof. Schinkel gave it a classical, almost Roman appearance, and he let his imagination loose in the interior, too—decorating one of the rooms as a Roman tent, with its walls and ceiling draped in striped canvas. ☎ *0331/969–4228.* ✉ *Guided tour DM 6.* ⊙ *Mid-May–mid-Oct., Tues.–Sat. 9–5.*

Römische Bäder (Roman Baths), **Orangerie**, and **Chinesisches Teehaus** (Chinese Teahouse), just north of the Schloss Charlottenhof on the path back to Sanssouci, were later additions to the park. Friedrich Wilhelm II built the Roman Baths (1836), while the teahouse was constructed in 1757 in the Chinese style, which was the rage then. The Orangerie (completed in 1860), with two massive towers linked by a colonnade, evokes an Italian Renaissance palace. Today it houses 47 copies of paintings by Raphael. The Italianate Peace Church (1845–48) houses a 12th-century Byzantine mosaic taken from an island near Venice. *Roman Baths:* ☎ *0331/969–4224.* ✉ *DM 3 (additional charge for special exhibition).* ⊙ *Mid-May–mid-Oct., Tues.–Sun. 10–5. Chinese Teahouse:* ☎ *0331/969–4222.* ✉ *DM 2.* ⊙ *Mid-May–mid-Oct., Tues.–Sun. 10–5. Orangerie:* ☎ *0331/969–189.* ✉ *Guided tour DM 5.* ⊙ *Mid-May–mid-Oct., Tues.–Sun. 10–5.*

NEED A BREAK? | Halfway up the park's Drachenberg Hill, above the Orangerie, stands the curious **Drachenhaus** (Dragon House), modeled in 1770 after the Pagoda at London's Kew Gardens and named for the gargoyles ornamenting the roof corners. It now houses a popular café.

Schloss Cecilienhof (Cecilienhof Palace), the final addition to Sanssouci Park, is equally exotic. Resembling a rambling, half-timbered country manor house, the Schloss Cecilienhof was built for Crown Prince Wilhelm in 1913 in a newly laid out stretch of the park bordering the Heiliger See, called the New Garden. It was here that the Allied leaders Truman, Attlee, and Stalin hammered out the fate of postwar Germany at the 1945 Potsdam Conference. ⊠ *Schloss Cecilienhof,* ☎ *0331/969–4244.* ⊑ *DM 8, including guided tour.* ⊙ *Apr.– Oct., Tues.–Sun. 9–5; Nov.–Mar., Tues.–Sun. 9–4.*

Potsdam-Stadt (Potsdam City) itself still retains the imperial character lent it by the many years during which it served as royal residence and garrison quarters. It shouldn't be overlooked. The central market square, the **Alter Markt** (Old Market Square) sums it all up: the stately, domed **Niko-laikirche** (St. Nicolai's Church; built in 1724), a square baroque church with classical columns; an **Ägyptischer Obelisk** (Egyptian obelisk) erected by Sanssouci architect von Knobelsdorff; and the officious facade of the old **Rathaus** (City Hall; built in 1755) with a gilded figure of Atlas atop the tower. Wander around some of the adjacent streets, particularly Wilhelm-Külz-Strasse, to admire the handsome restored burghers' houses.

Holländisches Viertel (Dutch Quarter) lies 3 blocks north of the Alter Markt. This settlement was built by Friedrich Wilhelm I in 1732 to induce Dutch artisans to settle in a city that needed migrant labor to support its rapid growth. (Few Dutch came, and the gabled, hip-roofed brick houses were largely used to house staff.) The Dutch government has promised to finance some of the cost of repairing the damage done by more than four decades of communist neglect.

Dining and Lodging

$$ ✕ **Juliette.** This small and intimate French restaurant in the
★   heart of the restored historic Holländisches Viertel has become one of Potsdam's most beloved eateries. The tiny place is in an old house with an open fireplace, cozy little windows, and low ceilings—the perfect place for a romantic dinner for two. Service may be somewhat slow, but the impeccable and delicious French cuisine more than makes up

for it, and the *charme* of the French waiters is as gratifying as the dishes. There are daily menus with three to four courses, including *Gebratene Gänsemastleber an Quittenpüree und Feldsalat* (fried taté de foie on quince puree and lamb's lettuce) or *Wildschweinrücken in Preiselbeerjus auf Rosenkohl und Maronen* (saddle of boar in cranberry juice on Brussels sprouts and chestnuts), for example. ✉ *Jägerstr. 39,* ☎ *0331/2701–791. Reservations essential. AE, V.*

$ ✕ **Preussischer Hof.** If you are up to genuine Berlin and Brandenburg cooking, try this restaurant in the historic heart of downtown Potsdam. The old building looks just like the city at the time when Frederick the Great ruled the country, and the dishes are just as hearty. Among the favorites of this popular and ever crowded place for locals and tourists alike are *Gepökeltes Eisbein auf Weinsauerkraut mit Erbspüree und Salzkartoffeln* (pickled hocks on wine sauerkraut with mashed peas and boiled potatoes), or *Entenbraten mit Apfelrotkohl und Kartoffelklössen* (roast duck with red cabbage and apples with potato dumplings). Don't be afraid of an upset stomach: some dishes include a *NordhäDoppelkorn,* German schnapps. If the relatively small menu doesn't appeal to you, ask for their specials of the week. ✉ *Charlottenstr. 11,* ☎ *0331/2700–762. Reservations essential. No credit cards.*

$$ 🏠 **Hotel am Luisenplatz.** This new and intimate hotel hides
★ a warm, upscale elegance and friendly, personal service behind a somber-looking (very Prussian, though) facade. The large rooms are decorated in typically Prussian colors—dark blue and yellow—and all have a bathtub. The biggest draw, however, is the hotel's location, offering a spectacular view of historic Luisenplatz and its restored Prussian city mansions. ✉ *Luisenplatz 5, D–14471,* ☎ *0331/971900,* 🖷 *0331/9719019. 25 rooms, 3 suites. AE, DC, MC, V.*

$$ 🏠 **Schlosshotel Charlottenhof.** This English country–style mansion is where Truman, Atlee, and Stalin drew up the 1945 Potsdam Agreement, and where Truman received news of the first successful atom bomb test, which took place on July 16, 1945. The hotel rooms are somewhat plain, although comfortable and adequately equipped. The Schloss is set in its own parkland bordering a lake and is a pleasant 15-minute stroll from Sanssouci and the city center. ✉ *Neuer Garten, D–14469,* ☎ *0331/37050,* 🖷 *0331/292–*

498. *36 rooms, 6 suites. Restaurant, room service, sauna. AE, D, MC, V.*

Potsdam A to Z

Arriving and Departing

Potsdam is virtually a suburb of Berlin, some 20 km (12 mi) southwest of the city center and a half-hour journey by car, bus, or S-bahn. City traffic is heavy, however, and a train journey is recommended. Perhaps the most effortless way to visit Potsdam and its attractions is to book a tour with one of the big Berlin operators (☞ Guided Tours *in* Berlin A to Z, *below*).

BY BOAT

Boats leave Wannsee, landing hourly, between 10 AM and 6 PM; until 8 PM in summer.

BY BUS

There is regular service from the bus station at the Funkturm, Messedamm 8 (U-1 U-bahn station Kaiserdamm).

BY CAR

From Berlin center (Str. des 17. Juni), take the Potsdamer Strasse south until it becomes Route 1 and then follow the signs to Potsdam. A faster way is taking the highway from Funkturm through Zehlendorf to Potsdam.

BY TRAIN

Take the S-bahn, either the S-3 or the S-7 line, to Potsdam Stadt (for the city and Schloss Sanssouci). Change there for the short rail trip to the Potsdam-Charlottenhof (for Schloss Charlottenhof) and Wildpark (for Neues Palais) stations. You can also take Bus 116 from Wannsee to the Glienecker Brücke, and then take a ride on the streetcar to Potsdam's Bassanplatz station. From there you can walk down Brandenburger Strasse to Platz der Nationen and on to the Green Gate, the main entrance to Sanssouci Park.

Guided Tours

All major sightseeing companies (☞ Guided Tours *in* Berlin A to Z, *below*) offer three- to four-hour-long tours of Potsdam and Sanssouci for DM 54. The **Potsdam Tourist Office** also runs two tours from April through October. Its three-hour tour, including Sanssouci, costs DM 35; the 1½-

hour tour of the city alone is DM 27 (☞ *Visitor Informa-tion, below*).

Visitor Information

The **Potsdam Tourist Office** (Potsdam Information) has in-formation on tours, attractions, and events, and also reserves hotel rooms for tourists. Their branch office at the Bran-denburger Strasse 18 also sells tickets for the Neues Palais theater. ⊠ *Friedrich-Ebert-Str. 5, Postfach 601220, D-14467 Potsdam,* ☎ *0331/275–680.* ☻ *Apr.–Oct., week-days 9–8, Sat. 10–6, Sun. 10–4; Nov.–Mar., weekdays 10–6, weekends 10–2.* ⊠ *Brandenburger Str. 18,* ☎ *0331/ 2708–100.* ☻ *Weekdays 10–6, Sat. 10–2.*

FRANKFURT AN DER ODER

Frankfurt an der Oder sits in its faded Prussian glory on the banks of the Oder River. Ninety percent of the historic center of town was destroyed in May 1945, not by Allied bombing but in a devastating fire that broke out after Ger-many's capitulation.

The **Rathaus** (City Hall), 100 yards west of the Oder, is the oldest building in town and also the most imposing. First mentioned in official records in 1348, the building has a 17th-century baroque facade that now looks out over the hustle and bustle of central Frankfurt. ⊠ *Marktpl.*

Kleist Gedenk- und Forschungsstätte (Kleist Memorial and Research Center) is an elegant and finely restored baroque structure situated on the Oder Riverbank behind City Hall. It's the world's only museum devoted to the great German writer Heinrich von Kleist (1777–1811). His works, no-tably the famous history play *Das Kätchen von Heilbronn* (source of one of Carl Orff's greatest compositions) and the comedy *der Zerbrochene Krug,* avoid all attempts at cat-egorization. The original manuscripts of both plays are in the museum, which traces Kleist's life and work with ex-emplary clarity and care. ⊠ *Faberstr. 7,* ☎ *0335/531– 155.* 🎫 *DM 4.* ☻ *Tues.–Sun. 10–5.*

Dining and Lodging

$$ ✕⊞ **Graham's.** This pension-hotel, run by a friendly staff, has a direct streetcar connection to much of the city. All the rooms have been modernized. The restaurant gives guests a choice of a rustic inn feel or a colorful café atmosphere. Both areas have the same menu, a variety of traditional German dishes and six different kinds of beer on tap. ⊠ *August-Bebel-Str. 11, D–15234 Frankfurt/Oder,* ☎ *0335/433–5429,* ☏ᴬˣ *0335/433–3991. 12 rooms, 4 apartments, all with shower. Restaurant. AE, MC, V.*

Frankfurt an der Oder A to Z

Arriving and Departing

BY CAR

Frankfurt an der Oder is 90 km (56 mi) east of Berlin, about an hour's drive. Head east on eastern Berlin's Landsberger Allee, joining the E–55 Ring-Autobahn and heading south until the Frankfurt/Oder turnoff. Exit at Frankfurt-Stadtmitte.

BY TRAIN

Trains depart every two hours from Berlin's Hauptbahnhof.

Visitor Information

Frankfurt Tourist Information, ⊠ *Karl-Marx-Str. 8a, D–15230 Frankfurt/Oder,* ☎ *0335/325–216,* ☏ᴬˣ *0335/22565.*

GERMAN VOCABULARY

Basics

English	German	Pronunciation
Yes/no	Ja/nein	yah/nine
Please	Bitte	*bit*-uh
Thank you (very much)	Danke (vielen Dank)	*dahn*-kuh (*fee*-lun-dahnk)
Excuse me	Entschuldigen Sie	ent-*shool*-de-gen zee
I'm sorry.	Es tut mir leid.	es toot meer lite
Good day	Guten Tag	*goo*-ten tahk
Good bye	Auf Wiedersehen	auf *vee*-der-zane
Mr./Mrs.	Herr/Frau	hair/frau
Miss	Fräulein	*froy*-line
Pleased to meet you.	Sehr erfreut.	zair air-*froit*
How are you?	Wie geht es Ihnen?	vee *gate* es *ee*-nen?
Very well, thanks.	Sehr gut, danke.	zair goot *dahn*-kuh
And you?	Und Ihnen?	oont *ee*-nen

Numbers

1	ein(s)	eint(s)
2	zwei	tsvai
3	drei	dry
4	vier	fear
5	fünf	fumph
6	sechs	zex
7	sieben	*zee*-ben
8	acht	ahkt
9	neun	noyn
10	zehn	tsane

Days of the Week

Sunday	Sonntag	*zone*-tahk
Monday	Montag	*moan*-tahk
Tuesday	Dienstag	*deens*-tahk
Wednesday	Mittwoch	*mit*-voah
Thursday	Donnerstag	*doe*-ners-tahk
Friday	Freitag	*fry*-tahk
Saturday	Samstag/ Sonnabend	*zahm*-stakh/ *zonn*-a-bent

Useful Phrases

Do you speak English?	Sprechen Sie Englisch?	*shprek*-hun zee *eng*-glish?
I don't speak German.	Ich spreche kein Deutsch.	ich *shprek*-uh kine doych
Please speak slowly.	Bitte sprechen Sie langsam.	*bit*-uh *shprek*-en-zee *lahng*-zahm
I am American/ British	Ich bin Amerikaner(in)/ Engländer(in)	ich bin a-mer-i-*kahn*-er(in)/ eng-glan-der(in)
My name is . . .	Ich heiße . . .	ich *hi*-suh
Yes please/No, thank you	Ja bitte/Nein danke	yah *bi*-tuh/*nine* dahng-kuh
Where are the restrooms?	Wo ist die Toilette?	vo ist dee twah-*let*-uh
Left/right	links/rechts	links/rechts
Open/closed	offen/geschlossen	O-fen/geh-*shloss*-en
Where is . . .	Wo ist . . .	*vo* ist
the train station?	der Bahnhof?	*dare bahn*-hof
the bus stop?	die Bushaltestelle?	*dee booss*-hahlt-uh-shtel-uh
the subway station?	die U-Bahn- Station?	dee oo-bahn-*staht*-sion
the airport?	der Flugplatz?	dare *floog*-plats
the post office?	die Post?	dee *post*
the bank?	die Bank?	dee *banhk*
the police station?	die Polizeistation?	dee po-lee-tsai-*staht*-sion
the American/ British consulate?	das amerikanische/ britische Konsulat?	dahs a-mare-i-*kahn*-ishuh/ *brit*-ish-uh cone-tso-*laht*
the Hospital?	das Krankenhaus?	dahs *krahnk*-en-house
the telephone	das Telefon	dahs te-le-*fone*
I'd like . . .	Ich hätte gerne . . .	ich *het*-uh gairn . . .
a room	ein Zimmer	ein *tsim*-er
the key	den Schlüssel	den *shluh*-sul
a map	eine Stadtplan	*I*-nuh *shtaht*-plahn
a ticket	eine Karte	*I*-nuh *cart*-uh
How much is it?	Wieviel kostet das?	vee-*feel cost*-et dahs?
I am ill/sick	Ich bin krank	ich bin *krahnk*
I need . . .	Ich brauche . . .	ich *brow*-khuh
a doctor	einen Arzt	*I*-nen artst
the police	die Polizei	dee po-li-*tsai*
help	Hilfe	*hilf*-uh
Stop!	Halt!	*hahlt*
Fire!	Feuer!	*foy*-er
Look out/Caution!	Achtung!/Vorsicht!	*ahk*-tung/*for*-zicht

Dining Out

A bottle of . . .	eine Flasche . . .	I-nuh *flash*-uh
A cup of . . .	eine Tasse . . .	I-nuh *tahs*-uh
A glass of . . .	ein Glas . . .	ein glahss
Ashtray	der Aschenbecher	dare *Ahsh*-en-bekh-er
Bill/check	die Rechnung	dee *rekh*-nung
Do you have . . .?	Haben Sie . . .?	*hah*-ben zee
Food	Essen	*es*-en
I am a diabetic.	Ich bin Diabetiker(in)	ich bin dee-ah-*bet*-ik-er
I am on a diet.	Ich halte Diät.	ich *hahl*-tuh dee-*et*
I am a vegetarian.	Ich bin Vegetarier(in)	ich bin ve-guh-*tah*-re-er
I cannot eat . . .	Ich kann . . . nicht essen	ich kan . . . nicht *es*-en
I'd like to order . . .	Ich möchte . . . bestellen	ich *mohr*-shtuh . . . buh-*shtel*-en
Menu	die Speisekarte	dee *shpie*-zeh-car-tuh
Napkin	die Serviette	dee zair-vee-*eh*-tuh
Separate/all	Getrennt/alles	ge-*trent*/*ah*-les
together	zusammen	tsu-*zah*-men

MENU GUIDE

English	German
Made to order	Auf Bestellung
Side dishes	Beilagen
Extra charge	Extraaufschlag
When available	Falls verfügbar
Entrées	Hauptspeisen
Home made	Hausgemacht
(not) included	. . .(nicht) inbegriffen
Depending on the season	je nach Saison
Local specialties	Lokalspezialitäten
Set menu	Menü
Lunch menu	Mittagskarte
Desserts	Nachspeisen
style	. . . nach . . . . Art
at your choice	. . . nach Wahl
at your request	. . . nach Wunsch
Prices are . . .	Preise sind . . .
Service included	inklusive Bedienung
Value added tax included	inklusive Mehrwertsteuer (Mwst.)
Specialty of the house	Spezialität des Hauses
Soup of the day	Tagessuppe
Appetizers	Vorspeisen
Is served from . . . to . . .	Wird von . . . bis . . . serviert

Breakfast

Bread	Brot
Roll(s)	Brötchen
Butter	Butter
Eggs	Eier
Hot	heiß
Cold	kalt
Decaffeinated	koffeinfrei
Jam	Konfitüre
Milk	Milch
Orange juice	Orangensaft
Scrambled eggs	Rühreier
Bacon	Speck
Fried eggs	Spiegeleier
White bread	Weißbrot
Lemon	Zitrone
Sugar	Zucker

Appetizers

Oysters	Austern
Frog legs	Froschschenkel
Goose liver paté	Gänseleberpastete
Lobster	Hummer
Shrimp	Garnelen
Crayfish	Krebs
Salmon	Lachs
Mussels	Muscheln
Prosciutto with melon	Parmaschinken mit Melone
Mushrooms	Pilze
Smoked . . .	Räucher . . .
Ham	Schinken
Snails	Schnecken
Asparagus	Spargel

Soups

Stew	Eintopf
Semolina dumpling soup	Grießnockerlsuppe
Goulash soup	Gulaschsuppe
Chicken soup	Hühnersuppe
Potato soup	Kartoffelsuppe
Liver dumpling soup	Leberknödelsuppe
Oxtail soup	Ochsenschwanzsuppe
Tomato soup	Tomatensuppe
Onion soup	Zwiebelsuppe

Methods of Preparation

Blue (boiled in salt and vinegar)	Blau
Baked	Gebacken
Fried	Gebraten
Steamed	Gedämpft
Grilled (broiled)	Gegrillt
Boiled	Gekocht
Sauteed	In Butter geschwenkt
Breaded	Paniert
Raw	Roh

When ordering steak, the English words "rare, medium, (well) done" are used and understood in German.

Fish and Seafood

Eel	Aal
Oysters	Austern
Trout	Forelle
Flounder	Flunder
Prawns	Garnelen
Halibut	Heilbutt
Herring	Hering
Lobster	Hummer
Scallops	Jakobsmuscheln
Cod	Kabeljau
Crab	Krabbe
Crayfish	Krebs
Salmon	Lachs
Spiny lobster	Languste
Mackerel	Makrele
Mussels	Muscheln
Red sea bass	Rotbarsch
Sole	Seezunge
Squid	Tintenfisch
Tuna	Thunfisch

Meats

Mutton	Hammel
Veal	Kalb(s)
Lamb	Lamm
Beef	Rind(er)
Pork	Schwein(e)

Cuts of Meat

Example: For "Lammkeule" see "Lamm" (above) + ". . . keule" (below)

breast	. . . brust
scallopini	. . . geschnetzeltes
knuckle	. . . haxe
leg	. . . keule
liver	. . . leber
tenderloin	. . . lende
kidney	. . . niere
rib	. . . rippe
Meat patty	Frikadelle

Meat loaf	Hackbraten
Cured pork ribs	Kasseler Rippchen
Liver meatloaf	Leberkäse
Ham	Schinken
Bacon and sausage with	Schlachtplattesauerkraut
Brawn	Sülze

Game and Poultry

Duck	Ente
Pheasant	Fasan
Goose	Gans
Chicken	Hähnchen (Huhn)
Hare	Hase
Deer	Hirsch
Rabbit	Kaninchen
Capon	Kapaun
Venison	Reh
Pigeon	Taube
Turkey	Truthahn
Quail	Wachtel

Vegetables

Eggplant	Aubergine
Red cabbage	Blaukraut
Cauliflower	Blumenkohl
Beans	Bohnen
green	*grüne*
white	*weiß*e
Button mushrooms	Champignons
Peas	Erbsen
Cucumber	Gurke
Cabbage	Kohl
Lettuce	Kopfsalat
Leek	Lauch
Asparagus, peas and carrots	Leipziger Allerlei
Corn	Mais
Carrots	Mohrrüben
Peppers	Paprika
Chanterelle mushrooms	Pfifferlinge
Mushrooms	Pilze
Brussels sprouts	Rosenkohl

Red beets	Rote Beete
Celery	Sellerie
Asparagus (tips)	Spargel(spitzen)
Tomatoes	Tomaten
Cabbage	Weißkohl
Onions	Zwiebeln
Spring Onions	Frühlingszwiebeln

Side Dishes

Potato(s)	Kartoffel(n)
fried	Brat . . .
boiled in their jackets	Pell . . .
with parsley	Petersilien . . .
fried	Röst . . .
boiled in saltwater	Salz . . .
mashed	. . . brei
dumplings	. . . klöße (knödel)
pancakes	. . . puffer
salad	. . . salat
Pasta	Nudeln
French fries	Pommes frites
Rice	Reis
buttered	Butter . . .
steamed	gedämpfter . . .

Condiments

Basil	Basilikum
Vinegar	Essig
Spice	Gewürz
Garlic	Knoblauch
Herbs	Kräuter
Caraway	Kümmel
Bay leaf	Lorbeer
Horseradish	Meerettich
Nutmeg	Muskatnuß
Oil	Öl
Parsley	Petersilie
Saffron	Safran
Sage	Salbei
Chives	Schnittlauch
Mustard	Senf

Artificial sweetener	Süßstoff
Cinnamon	Zimt
Sugar	Zucker
Salt	Salz

Cheese

Mild	Allgäuer Käse, Altenburger (goat cheese), Appenzeller, Greyerzer, Hüttenkäse (cottage cheese), Kümmelkäse (with caraway seeds), Quark, Räucherkäse (smoked cheese), Sahnekäse (creamy), Tilsiter, Ziegekäse (goat cheese).
Sharp	Handkäse, Harzer Käse, Limburger.
curd	frisch
hard	hart
mild	mild

Fruits

Apple	Apfel
Orange	Apfelsine
Apricot	Aprikose
Blueberry	Blaubeere
Blackberry	Brombeere
Strawberry	Erdbeere
Raspberry	Himbeere
Cherry	Kirsche
Grapefruit	Pampelmuse
Cranberry	Preiselbeere
Raisin	Rosine
Grape	Weintraube
Banana	Banane
Pear	Birne
Kiwi	Kiwi

Nuts

Peanuts	Erdnüsse
Hazelnuts	Haselnüsse
Coconut	Kokosnuß
Almonds	Mandeln
Chestnuts	Maronen

Desserts

. . . soufflé	. . . auflauf
ice cream	. . . eis
cake	. . . kuchen
Honey-almond cake	Bienenstich
Fruit cocktail	Obstsalat
Whipped cream	(Schlag)sahne
Black Forest cake	Schwarzwälder Kirschtorte

Drinks

chilled	eiskalt
with/without ice	mit/ohne Eis
with/without water	mit/ohne Wasser
straight	pur
room temperature	Zimmertemperatur
brandy	. . . geist
distilled liquor	. . . korn
liqueur	. . . likör
schnapps	. . . schnaps
Egg liquor	Eierlikör
Mulled claret	Glühwein
Caraway-flavored liquor	Kümmel
Fruit brandy	Obstler
Vermouth	Wermut

When ordering a Martini, you have to specify "gin (vodka) and vermouth," otherwise you will be given a vermouth (Martini & Rossi).

Beer and Wine

non-alcoholic	Alkoholfrei
A dark beer	Ein Dunkles
A light beer	Ein Helles
A mug (one quart)	Eine Maß
Draught	Vom Faß
Dark, bitter, high hops content	Altbier
Strong, high alcohol content	Bockbier (Doppelbock, Märzen)
Wheat beer with yeast	Hefeweizen
Light beer, strong hops aroma	Pils(ener)
Wheat beer	Weizen(bier)
Light beer and lemonade	Radlermaß
Wines	Wein
Rosé wine	Roséwein

Red wine	Rotwein
White wine and mineral water	Schorle
Sparkling wine	Sekt
White wine	Weißwein
dry	herb
light	leicht
sweet	süß
dry	trocken
full-bodied	vollmundig

Non-Alcoholic Drinks

Coffee	Kaffee
decaffeinated	koffeinfrei
with cream/sugar	mit Milch/Zucker
with artificial sweetener	mit Süßstoff
black	schwarz
Lemonade	Limonade
orange	Orangen . . .
lemon	Zitronen . . .
Milk	Milch
Mineral water	Mineralwasser
carbonated/non-carbonated	mit/ohne Kohlensäure
juice	. . . saft
(hot) Chocolate	(heiße) Schokolade
Tea	Tee
iced tea	Eistee
herb tea	Kräutertee
with cream/lemon	mit Milch/Zitrone

INDEX

X = restaurant, 🏨 = hotel

A

Accessibility concerns, *xxiii*
Addresses, *xii*
Ägyptischer Obelisk, *81*
Ägyptisches Museum, *34*
Airports, *xv–xvi*
Air travel
booking a flight, *xii*
carriers, *xii–xiii*
charters, *xiii*
check in and boarding, *xiv*
with children, *xix–xx*
complaint procedures, *xv*
consolidators, *xiii*
courier flying, *xiii–xiv*
cutting costs, *xiv*
enjoying the flight, *xiv–xv*
flying times, *xv*
luggage rules, *xxxi–xxxii*
Albrecht Wassersport, *67*
Alexanderplatz, *24*
Allgemeiner Deutscher Fahrrad-Club (ADFC), *66*
Alt-Cöllner Schankstuben X, *44–45*
Alte Nationalgalerie, *28*
Altes Museum, *28*
Alt-Luxemburg X, *40*
Ambulances, *xxv*
American Business Center, *18*
Anderes Ufer (kneipen), *61*
Animal Garden, *23*
Antikensammlung, *37*
Antiques shops, *71–72*
Art galleries and museums, *5*
historic eastern Berlin, *27–29*
outer Berlin, *34, 35, 36*
Potsdam, *77*
Tiergarten area, *19, 20*
Arts, the, *56–60*
ATMs, *xxx*
A-Trane Jazzclub, *63*
Auto clubs, *xviii*
Axel Sedlatzek (shop), *73*

B

Babylon (cinema), *58*
Baby-sitting services, *xix*

Bamberger Reiter X, *40*
Banks, *xvi*
Bar am Lützowplatz, *60*
Bar jeder Vernunft, *60*
Bars, *60*
Beaches, *67*
Beer, *4*
Bellevue Palace, *22*
Berggruen Collection, *35*
Berliner Antik- und Flohmarkt, *72*
Berliner Dom, *24–25*
Berliner Ensemble, *58–59*
Berliner Kunstmarkt, *72*
Berliner Rathaus, *25*
Berlin Festival Weeks, *56*
Berlin Hilton 🏨, *47*
Berlin Wall, *18, 35*
Beth Café X, *30*
Better Business Bureau, *xx*
Bikecity, *66*
Biking, *xxxvii, 66*
shipping bikes with airlines, *xv–xvi*
Blockhaus Nikolskoe X, *45*
Blub Badeparadies, *67*
Blue Note (nightclub), *64*
Boat trips, *xxvi*
to Potsdam, *83*
Bodemuseum, *29*
Bogner-Shop Zenker, *73*
Books in Berlin, *72*
Bookstores, *72*
Borchardt X, *40*
Brandenburger Tor, *17–18*
Brecht-Weigel-Gedenkstätte, *25–26*
Bristol Hotel Kempinski 🏨, *47, 50*
British Bookshop, *72*
Bucherer (shop), *73*
Buchhandlung Kiepert, *72*
Budapester Schuhe (shop), *73*
Bürgel-Haus, *71*
Business hours, *xvi*
Bus tours, *xxvi–xxvii*
Bus travel
city buses, *xxxvii–xxxviii*
long-distance service, *xxxviii*
to Potsdam, *83*
Butcher shops, *39*

C

Cabaret theaters, 59
Café Adler ✕, 18–19
Café Oren ✕, 45
Cameras and camcorders, xvi
Canal tours, xxvi
Car rentals, xvi–xvii
Car travel, xviii–xix
to Frankfurt an der Oder, 85
to Potsdam, 83
Casino Berlin, 61
Casinos, 61
Cecilienhof Palace, 81
Cemeteries, 25–26, 28
Centrum Judaicum, 30
Chamäleon Varieté, 60
Champussy (bar), 60
Chapeaux (shop), 72
Charlottenburg, 69
Charlottenburger Hof 🖭, 54
Charlottenburg Palace, 36–37, 67
Charter flights, xiii
Checkpoint Charlie, 18
Children and travel, xix–xx
attractions for children, 15, 59
Chinesisches Teehaus, 80
Christie's auction house, 72
Churches
historic eastern Berlin, 24–25, 27, 30–
31
Potsdam, 80
western downtown Berlin, 11, 14
City Hall (Frankfurt an der Oder),
84
City Hall (Potsdam), 81
Climate, xl
Clothing for the trip, xxxii
Clothing shops, 73–74
Computers, xvi
Concert halls, 57
Concerts, 56
Connection (disco), 62
Consolidators, xiii
Construction sites, 4
Consulates, xx
Consumer protection, xx
Coupon books, xxiv
Courier flying, xiii–xiv
Credit cards, xx, xxiv–xxv, xxx
Cultural Forum, 19–20

Currency, xxx–xxxi
Customs, xx–xxiii

D

Dahlem Museums, 34
Dance, 58
Debit cards, xxx
Dentists, xxv
Department store restaurants, 39
Department stores, 70
Deutsche Oper Berlin, 57
Deutscher Dom, 27
Deutsches Historisches Museum, 26
Deutsches Theater, 58
Deutschmarks, xxx–xxxi
Die Wühlmäuse, 59
Dining
Berlin, 15, 18–19, 26–27, 30, 31, 39–
45
Frankfurt an der Oder, 85
menu guide, 89–96
Potsdam, 80, 81–82
price chart, 39
tipping, xxxv
Disabled travelers, xxiii–xxiv
Discos, 62
Discounts and deals, xxiv–xxv
for senior citizens, xxxiii
Distel (cabaret), 59
Dorotheenstädtischer Friedhof, 25–26
Drachenhaus ✕, 80
Driver's licenses, xvii
Dussmann Kulturkaufhaus, 72
Duties, xx–xxiii

E

East Side Gallery, 35
Econtel 🖭, 54
Egyptian Museum, 34
Egyptian obelisk, 81
Eierschale (I) (jazz club), 63
Einstein Café ✕, 15
Electricity, xxv
Embassies, xx
Emergencies
police and medical, xxv–xxvi
road service, xviii
Emperor Wilhelm Memorial Church,
11, 14
English-language bookstores, 72

Estrel Festival Center, *57*
Estrel Residence Congress Hotel ⊠,
 52–53
Ethnographic Museum, *34*
Euro currency, *xxx*
Europa Center, *11, 69*
Exchanging money, *xxxi*
Exploring
Frankfurt an der Oder, 84
historic eastern Berlin, 23–32
*Kurfürstendamm and western
 downtown Berlin, 10–15*
outer Berlin, 32–37
Potsdam, 76–81
Tiergarten area, 15–23

F

Fahrrad Vermietung Berlin, *66*
Far Out (nightclub), *64*
Federal Senate, *25*
Fernsehturm, *24*
Film, *58*
Fischerinsel, *31*
Flöz (jazz club), *63*
Flughafen Tegel, *xv*
Forum Hotel Berlin ⊠, *52*
Four Seasons Hotel Berlin ⊠, *50*
Frankfurt an der Oder, *84–85*
Französischer Dom, *27*
Französischer Hof ✕, *41*
Frederick the Great, *76–77*
French Cathedral, *27*
Friedrichstadtpalast, *59–60*
Friedrichstadtpassagen, *26*
Friedrichstrasse, *26, 69*
Friends of Italian Opera, *59*

G

Galerie der Romantik, *36*
Galeries Lafayette, *26, 70*
Gasoline, *xix*
Gay and lesbian travel, *xxvi*
nightlife, 61–62
Gendarmenmarkt, *27*
German Cathedral, *27*
German History Museum, *26*
German vocabulary, *86–96*
Gift shops, *70–71*
Gipsformerei der Staatlichen Museen
 Preussischer Kulturbesitz, *71*
Golf, *66*

Graham's ✕ ⊠, *85*
Grand Hotel Esplanade ⊠, *50*
Granny's Step (shop), *73*
Green Door (kneipen), *62*
Green Forest, *35, 67*
Grips Theater, *59*
Grossbeerenkeller ✕, *41*
Grosser Sendesaal des SFB, *57*
Grunewald, *35, 67*
Guided tours, *xxvi–xxvii*
Potsdam, 83–84

H

Hackbarths (kneipen), *62*
Hafenbar (kneipen), *61*
Half-day itineraries, *5–8*
Hamburger Bahnhof, Museum für
 Gegenwart-Berlin, *27–28*
Hansa Theater, *59*
Hans Wurst Nachfahren, *59*
Harry's New York Bar, *60*
Hat shops, *72*
Haus am Checkpoint Charlie, *18*
Havel Lakes, *xxvi*
Health concerns, *xxvii*
Hebbel Theater, *59*
Hekticket office, *56*
Holidays, *xxvii*
Horseback riding, *66*
Hostels, *xxix–xxx, xxxiii–xxxiv*
Hotel Adlon Berlin ⊠, *50–51*
Hotel am Luisenplatz ⊠, *82*
Hotel Casino ⊠, *53*
Hotel Müggelsee ⊠, *53*
Hotels. ☞ Lodging
House at Checkpoint Charlie–The
 Wall Museum, *18*
Hugendubel (shop), *72*
Hugenottenmuseum, *27*
Humboldt-Universität, *32*

I

Insurance
for car rentals, xvii
*green card for driving in continental
 Europe, xviii–xix*
medical plans, xxvii, xxviii
travel insurance, xxvii–xxviii
Inter-Continental Berlin ⊠, *51*
Internationale Filmfestspiele, *58*
Itinerary suggestions, *5–8*

J

Jazz clubs, 63
Jewelry shops, 73
Jewish cultural center, 30
Jogging, 67
Jüdischer Friedhof, 28
Jüdisches Viertel, 30
Juliette ✕, 81–82

K

Kaiser-Wilhelm-Gedächtniskirche, 11, 14
Kammerspiele, 58
Kartoon (cabaret), 59
Kaufhaus des Westens, 14, 70
Kaufhof, 70
Kempinski Plaza, 70
Klein-Holz (shop), 74
Kleist Gedenk- und Forschungsstätte, 84
Knaack-Club, 63
Kneipen, 61, 62–63
Komische Oper, 57
Komödie, 59
Kongresshalle, 23
Königliche Porzellan Manufaktur, 71
Konzerthaus Berlin, 57
Konzertsaal der Hochschule der Künste, 57
Kramberg (shop), 73
Kronprinzenpalais, 28
Kulturforum, 19–20
Kumpelnest 3000 (kneipen), 62
Kunstgewerbemuseum, 20
Kurbel (cinema), 58
Kurfürstendamm, 14–15, 69–70

L

Landhaus Schlachtensee 🏠, 53
Language, xxviii–xxix
German vocabulary, 86–96
Leydicke (kneipen), 63
Libraries, 20, 25
Lindencorso building, 26
Lodging, xxix–xxx, 4–5
accessibility concerns, xxiii
Berlin, 47–54
children's accommodations, xix
discount reservations, xxv
Frankfurt an der Oder, 85
Potsdam, 82–83

price chart, 47
tipping, xxxv
Love Parade, 63–64
Luggage
airline rules, xxxi–xxxii
bikes as, xv–xvi

M

Mail service, xxx
Mann-O-Meter (gay gathering spot), 61
Marga Schoeller Bücherstube, 72
Märkisches Museum, 28
Martin-Gropius-Bau, 21
März ✕, 41, 44
Maxim Gorki Theater, 59
Medical assistance, xxv–xxvi
Medical plans, xxvii, xxviii
Menu guide, 89–96
Metropol Theater, 58
Mientus (shop), 73
Money, xxx–xxxi
Museum für Völkerkunde, 34
Museum für Vor- und Frügeschichte, 37
Museum Island, 28–29
Museum of Brandenburg, 28
Museum of Contemporary Art, 27–28
Museum of Pre- and Early History, 37
Museums, 5. ☞ Art galleries and museums
ancient world, 29, 34, 37
Berlin history, 28
Berlin Wall, 18
business hours, xvi
decorative arts, 20
ethnography, 34
in Frankfurt an der Oder, 84
German history, 26
in historic eastern Berlin, 26, 27, 28, 29
Huguenots, 27
Kleist, 84
musical instruments, 20
Nazi history, 21, 35
in outer Berlin, 34, 35
in Tiergarten area, 18, 20, 21
Museumsinsel, 28–29
Musicals, 57–58
Musikinstrumenten-Museum, 20

N

National Library, 20
Neue Nationalgalerie, 20
Neues Palais, 77, 80
Neue Synagoge, 29–30
Neue Wache, 32
Neuköllner Oper, 57
Nightclubs, 63–64
Nightlife, 5, 60–64
90 Grad (nightclub), 64
Nord-Süd-Tunnel, 23
Nouvelle (shop), 74

O

Observation towers, 24
Odeon (cinema), 58
Old Museum, 28
Old National Gallery, 28
Olympia-Schwimmstadion, 67
Opera, 57
Opera houses, 31
Opernpalais ✕, 31
Orangerie, 80
Outdoor activities, 66–67

P

Package deals, xxv, xxxvi–xxxvii
Packing, xxxi–xxxii
Palaces
historic eastern Berlin, 28
outer Berlin, 36–37
Potsdam, 76–77, 80–81
Tiergarten area, 22
Palast der Republik, 25
Paris Bar ✕, 40
Pariser Platz, 18
Parliament Building, 21–22
Passports, xxxii–xxxiii
Peace Church, 80
Peek und Cloppenburg (shop), 74
Pergamonmuseum, 29
Pharmacies, xxv–xxvi
Philharmonie mit Kammermusiksaal, 19–20, 57
Photography, xvi
Planet Hollywood ✕, 26–27
Podewil, 58
Police, xxv
Potsdam
arriving and departing, 83
dining, 80, 81–82

exploring, 76–81
guided tours, 83–84
lodging, 82–83
visitor information, 84
Potsdam Conference site, 81
Potsdamer Platz, 20–21
Potsdamer Platz Arkaden, 70
Potsdam-Stadt, 81
Prescription drugs, xxxii
Preussischer Hof ✕, 82
Preussischer Landtag, 21
Price charts
dining, 39
lodging, 47
Prince's Palace, 28
Prinz-Albrecht-Gelände, 21
Prussian State Legislature, 21
Public phones, xxxv

Q

Quasimodo (jazz club), 63

R

Rathaus (Frankfurt an der Oder), 84
Rathaus (Potsdam), 81
Red Town Hall, 25
Reichstag, 21–22
Reinhard's ✕, 44
Reitschule Stall-Schmitz, 66
Reitsportschule Haflinger Hof, 66
Reitsportschule Onkel Toms Hütte, 66
Restaurants. ☞ Dining
Riehmers Hofgarten 🏨, 54
Rio (shop), 73
Road conditions, xix
Rockendorf's ✕, 40
Römische Bäder, 80
Rosmarin-Karree building, 26
Rules of the road, xix

S

Sachsenhausen Gedenkstätte, 35
Sailing, 67
St. Hedwigskathedrale, 30
St. Marienkirche, 30–31
St. Nikolaikirche, 31
Sammlung Berggruen, 35
Sanssouci, 76–77
Schaubühne am Lehniner Platz, 58

Schauspielhaus, 27
Scheunenviertel, 30
Schiller-Theater, 58
Schloss Bellevue, 22
Schloss Cecilienhof, 81
Schloss Charlottenburg, 36–37, 67
Schloss Charlottenhof, 80
Schlosshotel Charlottenhof , 82–83
Schwuz (gay gathering spot), 61
Sculpture Collection, 34
Selbach (shop), 73
Senior-citizen travel, xxxiii
Shopping
  business hours, xvi
  department stores, 70
  gift shops, 70–71
  shopping districts, 69–70
  specialty stores, 71–74
Showtime Konzert- und
  Theaterkassen, 56
Siegessäule, 22
Silberstein (kneipen), 63
Skulpturensammlung, 34
Snack bars, 39
Sophienklub, 64
Sotheby's auction house, 72
Sowjetisches Ehrenmal, 22–23
Space Dream Musical Theater, 58
Special-interest tours, xxvii
Spielbank Berlin, 61
Sports, 66–67
Squash, 67
Staatsbibliothek, 20
Staatsoper Unter den Linden, 31,
  57
Staatsrat, 25
Stable Quarters, 30
Stachelschweine, 59
Stand-up snack bars, 39
State Opera, 31
Steigenberger Berlin ⊠, 51–52
Student travel, xxxiii–xxxiv
Subway system, xxxvii–xxxviii
Swimming, 67
Synagogues, 29–30

T

Tanzfabrik, 58
Taxis, xxxv, xxxviii
Tegel Airport, xv
Telephone service, xxxiv–xxxv

Templehof Airport, xv
Tennis, 67
Theater, 58–59
Theater am Halleschen Ufer, 59
Theater am Kurfürstendamm, 59
Theater des Westens, 57–58
Theaterkonzertkasse City Center, 56
Theater Zerbrochene Fenster, 59
Thürnagel ✗, 45
Ticket agencies, 56
Tiergarten, 23, 67
Tipping, xxxv
Tour operators, xxxv–xxxvii
  for disabled travelers, xxiii–xxiv
Toy shops, 74
Train travel, xxxviii–xxxix
  to Frankfurt an der Oder, 85
  to Potsdam, 83
Travel agencies
  choosing an agency, xxxix
  for disabled travelers, xxiii–xxiv
  student-oriented agencies, xxxiv
  for tour bookings, xxxv–xxxvi
Travel clubs, xxiv
Travel insurance, xxvii–xxviii
Tucci ✗, 40–41
Turmstuben ✗, 44

U

Uhland-Passage, 70
Unter den Linden, 31–32
U.S. government travel information,
  xxxix

V

Variety shows, 59–60
VAU ✗, 41
Victory Column, 22
Visitor information
  Berlin, xl
  Frankfurt an der Oder, 85
  Potsdam, 84
Vocabulary words, 86–96
Volksbühne am Rosa-Luxemburg-
  Platz, 59

W

Waldbühne, 57
Walking tours, xxvii
Weather, xl
Weigel, Helene, 25

Wertheim (department store), *70*
Westin Grand Hotel ⊞, *52*
Wilmersdorfer Strasse, *69*
Windsurfing, *67*
Wintergarten, *60*
Women, visitor information for, *xl*

Z

Zitadellen-Schänke ✕, *44*
Zoologischer Garten, *15*
Zur Letzten Instanz ✕, *45*
Zur Rippe ✕, *44*

WHEREVER
YOU TRAVEL,
*H*ELP IS NEVER
FAR AWAY.

From planning your trip to providing travel assistance along the way, American Express® Travel Service Offices are always there to help you do more.

Berlin

American Express Travel Service
Uhlandstr 173
(49) (30) 8845880

American Express Travel Service
Friedrichstrasse 172
(49) (30) 238 4102-9

American Express Travel Service
Bayreuther Strasse 37
(49) (30) 2149830

American Express Travel Service
Mullerstr. 176
(49) (30) 462 3072

Travel
www.americanexpress.com/travel

**American Express Travel Service Offices
are located throughout Germany.**